CW00524970

MANDA
LIFE COACH

PAULA TOOTHS

1st Edition – Revised in May.2013

(Black and White Special Edition)

London – U.K.

The original package contains only this book.

Please check on paulatooths.com on how to purchase the deck of 80 mandalas' cards.

FOR MY BABY BOY

A MESSAGE TO THE WORLD

"Disabled is the one who cannot change their life, accepting others impositions or the society they live in, without any awareness that they are responsible for their own destiny.

Crazy is the one who does not want to be happy with what they have.

Blind is the one who cannot see the others dying of cold, starvation, misery and only has eyes for their own petty problems and little sorrows.

Deaf is the one who doesn't have the time to hear a friend, or a brother's plea, as they're always rushing to work and wants to make sure they have their pennies at the end of the month.

Mute is the one who cannot speak out their feelings and hide behind the mask of hypocrisy.

Paralytic is the one who cannot walk towards the ones who need help.

Diabetic is the one who cannot be sweet.
Dwarf is the one who doesn't allow Love to grow."

- Mario Quintana

INDEX

INTRODUCTION

The cards have been following me since I was a small child. Looking back I would have been about four years old and I vividly recollect my beloved grandmother taking me in her arms and explaining to me that she had a gift she needed to pass onto someone, but it needed to be someone special who could be trusted with this special secret.

I recall being full of curiosity as I sat on the corner of the bed in my grandmother's room and quietly waited there as she drew the curtains and lit a candle. She made her way over and sat next to me on the edge of the bed and clasped my hands in hers whilst looking into my eyes. Still smiling she whispered to me "the cards have picked you" and as I listened in silence she leaned across to the side of the bedstead and reached for a velvet pouch resting on top of her music box.

My grandmother then leaned over and picked up a cigarette which she lit from the candle, as I glanced around, having never spent much time in her bedroom, I noticed piles and piles of books. There was a wide variety of titles but what I did notice was that there were more about philosophy than any other. I remember thinking this was interesting as I had only ever seen her reading old romance novels when she was in the garden or around the house.

Grandma looked towards me and smiled. She looked into my eyes and asked me to relax, to be empty of any thoughts and to close my eyes and be calm.

As I sat there in silence I could hear the sound of an old clockwork music box begin to chime, I opened just one eye to glance over and could see my grandmother shuffling the cards as the ballerina danced on the music box. I closed my eye again and relaxed and as I did I could just hear the old music box imagining each of its rusted cogs turning in time.

It's a moment I never forgot and to this day I can still close my eyes and smell the candle and cigarette smoke mixed together.

As I lay there quite tranquil now my grandmother spoke and asked me to think about the things I wanted most in my life, what future I dreamed of, at such a young age I think I spent more energy squeezing my eyes closed than processing the situation in front of me.

I was almost sleeping when the next thing I heard was my grandmother counting back from 3 to 1; I wasn't sure where she had even started. I opened my eyes and sat up as my grandmother looked into my eyes again pausing for a moment before speaking, "welcome to your new world"

I sat there in silence looking around, not entirely sure what to expect, not sure if this had been a strange game we had played but nothing seemed different other than my grandmother was stood up now away from the bed and she started to speak to me. She said phrases about how to live a good life, quoting from the many books she had around the room, as an adult now I recognize the quotes from such greats as Albert Einstein and Platao.

As I sat up on the bed I looked forward and just below my feet were a set of playing cards laid out in lines. With great patience we spent the next long hours sitting there as she dissected each and every card and the meanings behind them, taking great care not to miss anything. Sometimes she spent extra time going over the same cards again and again just to be certain I had fully understood each one.

I remember feeling like my brain had been over stretched with all this information but I think my grandmother could see this and told me that I should try to relax a little as the cards would speak to me when the time was right.

It is my understanding that the cards are passed through the family from generation to generation and it was a natural order that they be passed onto me.

Having spent the best part of the day digesting what was being told to me and at such a young age I think it was all a little too much for me, maybe a little too intense and after the day had ended I began avoiding the cards altogether until many years had passed.

Having grown into an adult and with the passing of my grandmother, the most vivid memory I have of her was this day we spent together. It wasn't until many years later I started to feel a desire for the cards. I ignored this for much of the time and I had my own child and a very busy life, but the desire became more like a hunger that was burning inside, a thirst I could never quench until I had to give in and read the cards. The very same cards that belonged to my grandmother still wrapped in the dark red pouch.

It was my belief that I was being asked to help others understand, to help with guidance both spiritually and physically using the knowledge I have garnered over the years with my homeopathy, herbalism and nutrition. I have been reading the cards and gathering information with my studies for the last five years and now feel ready to take the next step.

My remaining grandmother has since taught me about the flowers and the aroma blends, the meanings and the uses for all. I was also fortunate that she showed me how to practice Reiki and the many natural benefits it has on our system. I have been taught mantra and how to connect with nature and all its wonders it has to offer.

My mother is a physician and excels in quantum physics and astronomy; she was the one who taught me how to use intuition and how to use our guide light, to feel love instead of fears. She showed me the natural powers of grains and spices and how to play with nutrition in your favour.

I believe the best blue print from my mother is the self-affirmation beliefs and the techniques of daily repetition of your words about our desires in life, the absolute power of thought.

My father spent every day from a young age coaching me and teaching me what coaching was before I knew what coaching was, with his sharp questions and how he made me look into my own mind for the answer, how to control my mind without limitations.

Natural medicine and divination has always been present with my life throughout our family's history and from a very young age I was aware of the huge benefits and success it has to offer.

I now realize I have been trained and guided from birth with all this knowledge over the years and have been placed into a fortunate position where I can pass onto others. Obviously there are some secrets that will remain so and only be passed within the family as it has always been, but what remains is an abundance of knowledge I can pass onto you with the hopes it will fulfil and enrich your lives as it has done for myself and my family.

I hope you all enjoy this trip and guide,

Love and blessings

Paula Tooths

"If you want to learn something,

Read about it.

If you want to understand about something,

Write about it.

If you want to master something,

Teach it!"

∞ Yogi Bhajan

HISTORY

§ DIVINATION

'Future' reading is an ancient practice used to understand the past, set the present and review the future. Some people believe this is a valuable practice and try to incorporate it into their lives. However, the more sceptical believe it is nothing more than "hocus pocus" and refuse to embrace the possibilities of its existence. Time continues to pass as with every aspect of life but now we are finding that more and more scientists and physicians are integrating these past methods into the modern world of medicine and incorporating these alternative treatments into their practices.

There is no doubt that within some families there is still a great volume of treatments hidden from everyday life and kept within their own circles. These treatments could be used to enhance our times and cure a great many people, but the sceptics ridicule the idea and actively prevent this from happening. These alternative treatments will always be shunned by certain powers that in turn place doubt into the minds of the public. Politics and corruption play a large part in this and the subject is too involved to discuss here, however if you are reading this then you are one of the many who already have belief in this and have not had your head turned by false media.

Divination has a Latin etymology "divinus" which translates into 'be inspired by god' which in turn when translated into modern English simply means 'divine'.

Without any doubt astrology was the first divination system, as soon as human beings could count the moons and time the seasons along with watching the movements of the stars they created the roots of astrological science. Early evidence to support this was found in drawings in caves and various monuments created by past generations in the Baghdad area. Some scientists believe that these date back more than twenty-five thousand years. The history of divination traces back to the third millennium BC to the Chinese dynasty where the eight trigrams "ba gua", read in the "book of change", (also known as the old Chinese text by Fu Xi), was found related to the Taostic cosmology 'the sixty four hexagrams of "I"' and most recently refered to as i-ching by Confucius.

Following the history of the Geomancy (a method of reading the future using math) in Egypt and other Arabic countries, research has found links with it within Indian texts. This points to the understanding that future reading dates back even further than our recorded knowledge in the subject. In the same period of time in West Africa and other countries on the same continent there have been further discoveries of the first signs of Ifa which in turn gave origin to afro natural medicine and well known religions such like voodoo, Umbanda and Candomble.

In the second millennium there were signs of the existence of a 'wild woman' of the Biscayan civilization. She could speak in the name of god using drawings of mythical people to guess the weather in simple combinations of dry and wet and hot and cold. Later the same figure from this time appears in the Ottoman Empire and strongly within the Turkish Islamic civilization.

In the first millennium BC, divination using cards is recorded in the Assyrian empire. However, card reading had been spread within printing history throughout the fifteenth century whilst at the same time in northern Europe; the use of runes was born using the gothic alphabet. These were actually the same words used to translate the bible. And finally we find that in the records of the Pythia (or pythoness) that as far as records will merit, is the idea that all women possess what is commonly referred to as a woman's sixth sense. In the past they may have been accused of being witches or part of the wiccan faith.

The oracles appeared named after a Latin word "Orare" meaning to speak. This shows in history that there were few people who were granted an audience with people who desired to know the truth, obviously depending on which area of the world you were in would depend on the methods used to tell the histories to those who had had asked the questions. Often this would involve people being sat on the 'Mandala' where the speaker would be talk in the name of god to others with various instruments. It would also involve rituals and in some cultures there were sacrifices. With rituals the story would be told involving stones, bones, drawings and calendars etc.

All the religions without any exceptions have some link with divination, the bible mentions the vision of Abraham, and the Catholic Church only abolished pagan and their practices in the year 692. The Hebrew bible clearly states in Leviticus 19.26 'you must not practice divination or soothsaying'. The Israelite beliefs point to divination by urim and thummin classified as cleromancy, which was used to orientate the future.

Islamic history points to the use of coins to obtain simple yes or no answers and the ornithomancy would seek answers from the songs of the birds and the Arabic tarot.

So many different forms of divination have been created, and each, within its own right, is as equally brilliant as the others. There is no bad divination system, only those who are inter-operating them for others and whether they are truly focused on receiving the messages as they are presented. Those who have the control and dedication to converse spiritually on those levels should achieve accuracy and success.

§ DIVINATION CARDS

Oracle cards are without doubt the most commonly used divination tools used to gain insight. These cards carry pictures, symbols and sometimes even words or numbers.

As mentioned in the previous text about the history of Divination, handmade cards are often in use and have been since the first millennium BC; however it wasn't until the fifteenth century when the printing press was invented that it really became recognized on a much larger scale.

The strings or "playing money cards" are credited as a Chinese invention it was only after the nineteenth century they were introduced to the rest of the world. The belief is that the practice is between 3000 – 5000 years old. The cards appeared in Spain most likely from that of a traveller before moving on to the region of Marseille in France. As with all things, they progressed and grew in volume and soon consisted of four sets of fourteen, commonly known as our playing card set. It is believed that Witches in that era where often found to be reading the cards to kings and princes which later gave set to the tarot or as it was known there the Marseille Tarot.

That said, the very first decks recognized by the spiritual society were those called the 'Trionfi' and later the 'Tarocco' and were credited to Milan, Italy, in the fourteenth century.

The composition of that deck was not unfamiliar to the classic tarot used then. The first set was called "Major Enigmas" with twenty-two cards corresponding to twenty-two letters of the Hebrew Alphabet. These again were extremely similar to the twenty-two cards of Major Arcana which we all know. The second set were called 'Minor Trunfos', which contain four sets of fourteen figures, so again similar to standard playing cards and had equal logic to the "Minor Arcana. Practitioners and researchers believe that Tarocco's first twenty-two are directly related to the science of astronomy but continue to be a massive enigma. Those who created these cards did not leave any clues and they cannot tracked any further back than the seventeenth century. The twenty-two "Major Arcana" gave origin to the Hebrew "Kabala".

Tarot cards fuelled a French occult revival and in 1888 two magical orders were formed, the "Cabalistic" order of the Rosy Cross in France and the "Hermetic" order of the Golden Down in England, it should be noted Golden Down follow the principles of "Thoth" cards.

Later psychology integrated the ideas. The physiologist Carl Jung attached much importance to the symbolism of Tarot.

Other groups of researchers simply believe that the modern Tarot is merely a reproduction of the hieroglyphical keys to life as used in the Islamic community in Egypt, which is a common myth.

Serious Historians, generally speaking have little or no desire to be associated with future telling or other divinatory subjects, but relate the history to art. To them divination cards are a product of mystery and fairy tale.

Tarot Cards contain unique symbolism, which cannot be traced to one specific culture. Different packs were designed to read different things as such Logic, Greek mythology, religion, geography and even art of carving meat and fish.

The cards have become so popular that they are created now on a global scale, But the Divination cards first appearance and who created them will always be they questions asked. This in itself will always be an enigma.

MANDALA ORACLE

After thirty long years of holding the divination cards for myself, having been passed them from my grandmother, I have been studying them and all they have to offer. I finally realised it was my inner guide that was pushing me to share my teachings and help others understand this world. It has been a long and sometimes confusing journey but now I feel comfortable to teach whoever desires to understand them. I'm ready and spiritually prepared to help them on this journey of self conquer.

After much study and taking into account all my all of my experience and the facts I have learned, I have now devised a system that I have tested with groups of people. This coupled with our natural sixth sense, it was possible to help others with their lives and assist them in avoiding difficult situations by finding the part of their inner being that required help and re balancing their lives.

I have being practicing this system to great success now for the past four years and had a desire to create some cards; I needed some help here as my artistic skills leave a lot to be desired.

I don't believe that you can shake the cards off if you get a reading that worries you. What is important however, are that some small things are unavoidable and are placed in our life's path so that as it passes it will build and create a stronger you for the future.

Broadening my mind as not only a person but as a coach helping people to think outside the box, I would advise people play with a larger set of cards than the classical Tarot.

In my experience it is best to play the cards twice for one individual and this will be explained in the following text.

As a ritual I will always light some candles and incense, this will allow your soul to invigorate you as you prey to your mantras and affirmations, then when you are ready ask the person in front of you to repeat my words. I also like to remember that when picking my choices for aromas, herbs, music and incense is dependent on the person I have in front of me, I will always allow my soul to guide me here so we can get the best mindset for the person.

Together we will do a mini section of guided meditation whilst relaxed in the natural lotus position, I will start with cards on the floor, I do prefer to be closes to the earth and this with me barefoot naturally appeals to me.

HOW TO PLAY

1st BLOOM

Shuffle the set of cards until you feel in sync with them. It will become easier over time to understand the feeling of the cards controlling your hands. Open the cards and place them in a circle position on the ground, much like the circle of life.

I have created eight slices as an overview, where I have placed them as though I were watching from a helicopter above; As you become more familiar, you will learn the splits and positions that are best suited to you.

2ND BLOOM

Once you have reviewed the cards in front of you and established knowledge of that person, you need to discover what they are trying to tell you with regards to worries and problems that they are facing and what they hope will come to pass soon. You will be guided to help them understand the 'why' and then guide them to a solution. This will allow you to help them with their situation and steer them onto the right path, whilst confronting the past they have experienced. This has most likely left deep routed scars on their soul which when addressed will transform and invigorate them.

For the second Bloom

- Once again shuffle the cards until you feel instinctively that it is time to stop.
- Ask the person you are reading for to cut the cards three times. With each cut, they should move the cards from the pile you hold, toward themselves placing them on top of each other and therefore creating a new single pile.
- Taking the cards once again, start from the top and deal them one at a time. Placing them face down creating a circle anticlockwise, from right to left, placing the final card in the centre of the circle.
- Starting from the first card dealt and reading from right to left, the first five cards represent their present. The next card represents their distant past and the next one represents their recent past.
- The following three cards represent the things in their life that they are blind to.
- The next two cards represent their near future.
- The next three represent their distant future.
- The last three in the circle represent their message from the cards.
- The final card in the centre of the circle represents the ego, or the self. This is the centre of the Mandala.

Once you are familiar with the way the cards are shuffled and the order in which they are dealt for representation, the physical shape of the placement can be adjusted to suit your own methods.

It will take you some time and practice to fully understand and digest this system but once you are comfortable with the placement and representations of the cards, you can move to the next section where I will explain the meaning behind each card and what it represents.

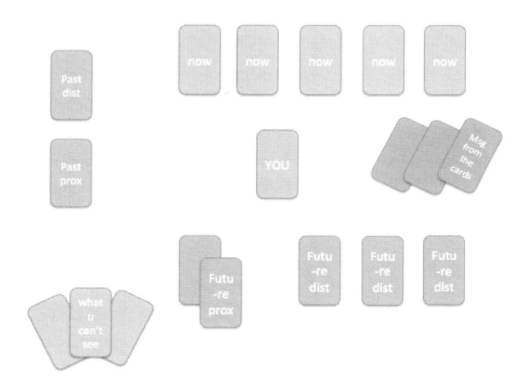

MANDALA CARDS

As mentioned at the start of the chapter, I could not do the art myself even after all these years and no real solution to carry off with my "Laminas"

Years have passed where I would involve myself then remove myself and such like until I was told that unless I fulfilled my true destiny my life could never is complete as intended.

On one particular day I couldn't have been more shocked, I had been meditating for a brief moment and after finishing made my way into the lounge area where my small son was playing. He was sat there on the sofa with his computer tablet in hand and as I walked over to give him a kiss I looked down and saw he was drawing a wonderful bright picture, I looked on memorized as he tried to explain what it was he was drawing? He was able to print the pictures using the easy print button, I sat there for some moments while he continued to print, once all were in hand placed them on the floor so each could be looked at clearly.

This was at a time I needed to reduce my working hours so as to care for him after his diagnosis, it was always a challenge as he didn't communicate very well however he was an absolute whiz at technology and often he is with his computer tablet or computer. Academically speaking he was far superior for his age it was just he has struggled to control his thoughts and feelings and how to express them.

He continued to make his Mandalas and we would print them and cut them out together.

Time passed quickly and soon we had collected the entire 80 cards required, with these in hand I started to use them on a regular basis, the more I used the cards the more I had a desire to use them. It reminds me of the old Buddhist proverb "when the student is ready the teacher will appear" I believe now that I am more than ready to share my life experience and teachings.

GROUP 1 – GRAN SECRETO

"The simple things are also the most extraordinary things, and only the wise can see them." - Paulo Coelho

1 – MAGUS

- Inspired in the idea of infinity, the card Magus is the very first card of the group 'gran secreto' and brings up the idea that the word had been created as a magical sentence. This card in the modern times can be translated more as theology, and who holds the mystery of the world.

- Magus represents the personal power, the high self-confidence, the infinite conscience, immanence, focus and concentration. This alchemist can be sharp, precocious and manipulative. A natural illusionist whom, with no effort, gains followers from whoever passes it by. As suggested the first Hebrew letter 'Aleph' and also in the many years in the past was the meaning of this card for so many categories of readers and exoteric, it can be translated as a natural leader.

- Usually selfish massively Skilled, dynamical and charismatic, the "magus" makes what they want happen.

- This card uses as keywords, action, movement, energy, practicality, initiative, creativity, and attitude.

- With this card, I recommend a homeopathic / Bach flower medicine called Vine, which helps to open the heart and to remind the personality that positive leadership is the result of a partnership between the heart and the mind.

- Aromatherapy can have a great impact. With this card, I would recommend notes of cinnamon and myrrh to accent "magus" powers with healing and transformation. With this card on the main position, I also would advise black pepper corns everywhere, as aroma, as spice, to make drinks and even decoration.

Magus Mantra: 'I can heal my past. I'm my best self now. I'm powerful enough to transform my destiny and make a magical future' - from Paula Tooths' #mymantratoday

2 – PĀPISSA

- This card in so many different studies and terminologies was inspired by Pope Joan, who in the Middle Ages, pretended to be a man to become part of the higher power of the church. The history point was the legend that this was the first female to run the world politically and religiously. Other studies have the belief that the second card from the major arcana was a devotion to the Egyptian goddess Hathor, who means to the Islamic motherhood, love and its symbol of female.

- This card represents the wise female, guardian of the kingdom knowledge, the person who knows more than the rest of her community. Is the woman who is ready to teach and guide.

- Knowingness, the Papissa has the understanding about love and can valuate relationships. This figure can also have the interpretation of unconditional pure love.

- Using common sense and full of intuition, the Papissa has wisdom enough to judge lightly and come to be the best decision with serenity.

- Because of all her power, easily she can leave without that of a man and involved in secrets, she is hard to relate to because nobody can read her mind.

- So many times introspective, considered a guardian of mythic, she has extra power and is the one who know the words by reading people's eyes.

- With this card, I recommend a flower remedy to help to grow communication. Water violet is the best pick and will keep the Papissa on the right road.

- Aromatherapy can be very helpful and the use of clary sage, to keep her intuition strong, without extra explanations, but certain that she will always pick the right way. A good and fresh cup of tea crafted with orange peel and cinnamon can guarantee the female powers she has already.

Papissa Mantra: 'I have all the strength to choose the right answers because they are all collected right there, inside my heart.' - From Paula Tooths' #mymantratoday

3 – IMPERĀTRIX

- Inspired by the queen of heaven, this card has the desire for life under all other circumstances.

- Similar to the third card from the major arcana in the classic tarot, the Imperatrix represents a young woman, full of beauty and power. Holding the planets fertility, she is the creator, the woman who looks after her creation. Some scientists deeply believe this figure is a reproduction of sacrifices to the Greek goddess of harvest - Demeter. And other researches bring to the image of Venus, the Roman Goddess that represents love, sex, beauty and manipulation.

- Imperatrix is the person who commands the desires; with delight she is a choreographer of sensuality and a mother of Nature. It's also is the symbolism that takes the attention to the health

- Full of pleasure, the Imperatrix is the sign of fertility and material prosperity. The keyword for this Mandala is abundance and comfort.

- I highly advise Willow, the last flower remedy from Dr. Edward Bach list, just to guarantee the natural balance. This remedy will also underline and increase her already existent powers.

- Fennel tea is a good pick to endure the power and can be easily added to food and drinks.

- Another important fact that I observed in the recent years is that with this card, the use of mix of roses in aromatherapy just makes the enchantment become true. It can be in baths, showers, perfumes, oils or even teas to odorize the house.

Imperatrix Mantra: 'I am so grateful for all I already have. I fell blessed for the life I have now' - From Paula Tooths' #mymantratoday

4 - IMPERĀTOR

- Inspired in the father of the father and sometimes mentioned as Zeus from the Greek Mythology, he is able to create order out of chaos by carefully categorizing his thoughts and mapping out what needs to be done to solve the problem.

- As the main masculine symbol, his desire is to rule the world he is in, but a big lesson he never have learnt is that he needs to relax about situations which he has no control.

- The Imperator established a solid family line and is often seen as the patriarch, offers guidance in his advices and always has a solution from his Kim group. This powerful man is also full of serenity, and complementing the Imperatrix offers comfort and security.

- This card owns the authoritarianism of the deck, but read in the negative vows, it will represent domination, manipulation, excessive control; it can be lose a few yards on the front, also a person who doesn't have flexibility in a very rigid value.

- Here we also will see the 'minister of affairs' and we can considerate as keywords tradition, conservative, leader, egocentrism; but full of order and organization, remembering that his structure is in the command.

- In the kitchen, I highly recommend more use of oregano, as much as borage on the physical body (skin).

- An interesting mix I would prescribe with this card read, is wild rose with rock water; for at least 3 weeks.

Imperator Mantra: 'I do not control the world and I accept that I can help others to improve their selves as much as I help myself.' - From Paula Tooths' #mymantratoday

5 - ANTITES

- This trump dates back to the inspiration of the Mycenaean ages, in particular to the leader of the mystical schools in the Elysium in Ancient Greece and their rituals of initiation, later studies pointed to the God Jupiter.

- This card means the strongest spiritual and military leader. Usually, this card shows a situation, which involves knowledge, expertise and education. This figure also can represent the new system, new life with maturity that in resume is the new with the wise of the old.

- The Antites is powerful and brings with him, discipline and intuition. Good psychologist and responsible not just for the spiritual and military advices, but probably for the whole community subjects.

- Apart all the religious and/ or spiritual words we could fit for this lamina, we also could apply as a keywords as well conformity, faith, routine and ritual.

- Garlic and clove are recommended to add in the diet, not necessarily together. In aromatherapy, vanilla is an interesting essential oil that can help to endure the power indicated in here; it be used in showers, baths, sprays, into perfumes notes or even in fabric conditioners.

- The best pick of Dr. Bach's Flowers Remedy is Oak, which will help with the flexibility and the other aspects of this figure.

Antites Mantra: 'I don't believe I need to control the universe to find respect. I search the truth and because I respect myself the others respect me and believe on my faith.'

- From Paula Tooths' #mymantratoday

6 – AMANTĒS

- Amantes is a card, which the sciences believe was created after the Archangel Raphael, after nominated as cupid, who blessed all with magic powers, the lovers.

- This card represents the relationships, the carnal physical love meaning as a portal from the young years to the adult life, when technically we are aloud to the desires. This card can also mean the twins, with their balance, sharing forces.

- Full of sexuality, temptations, desire and pleasure, this lamina brings on it the doubt, the union, the choices and opportunities.

- Keywords for this figure are physical attraction, principles, passion and humanism.

- I would recommend adding pink peppercorn and saffron on the diet and Ginger that can be used in the nutrition in aromatherapy. Following with aromas, I must advice Neroli and Patchouli.

- The best flower medicine is a blend of Cerato, to be sure that the intuition you will find is the best answers and hold the best choices, with confidence.

Amantes Mantra: 'I believe in my heart. I am very confident that the best choice will occur to my journey naturally.' - From Paula Tooths' #mymantratoday

7 - CURRUS

- I personally believe the version of history, which says the card Currus, was originated on the old Hindu scripts where it mentions the God Krishna who takes another God – Arjuna, to illuminate his thoughts and his way, with the symbolism of a warrior driving a chariot triumphantly home.

- The Currus always will be orientated by a strong minded driver, who is highly self confident and very assertive.

- This trump represents the possibility of traveling through the mysteries of the universe, it means the guide to find the way, but it's more about the struggles we have with ourselves and with life. But there shows a good touch with management.

- The Chariot is a very complex card when it comes to defining it. Brave, egocentric and victorious figure, the Currus fits with some keywords which when

43

glued to your intuition can make it a better reading – Energy, success, willpower, conquest, and discipline. Anxiety and Inflexibility can be part of it path.

- Recommendations to add marjoram to the kitchen and notes of pine aroma make full potential this card.

- A good prescription for this lamina from Dr. Bach List is Gentian Flower Remedy. Just as a rule, it will cover the courage to front easily and with positivity in the future.

Currus Mantra: 'I make legitimate efforts; I am worth the advance. Triumph guides my future.'– From Paula Tooths' #mymantratoday

8 - IŪSTITIA

- This card, without doubt has all the attribution to the Greek goddess Athena. She is a hero, who is patroness of justice, the main character in history for wisdom, warfare and divine intelligence.

- This card represents the decisions, the objective mind to be impartial to take the best judgment. The Iustitia comes full of intellect and realism, which using logical thoughts, always has the reason and knows how to take the rational position.

- Traditional and strong, this trump brings all the conservatives ideas, the analytical protocol and as a cold creature, the universal responsibility to be fair. Never uses the heart but always the experience of jurisprudence.

- The main affirmative posture of this card is that it always will have compensation to those ones who persist with hard work and treat life with honesty.

- Common keywords for Iustitia are balance, equality, truth, karma, justice, accountability, integrity and dignity.

- Adding Olive oil in the kitchen is recommended to provide equilibrium as well in aromatherapy a mix of lavender and chamomile to relax the cold heart feelings and bring up the divine intelligence to be sure that illuminated decisions will be taken.

- I generally choose Scleranthus Flower Medicine with this lamina to propose stability and guarantee the balance to the system.

Iustitia Mantra: 'I am strong and illuminated. I rely on my heart to provide fairness. When I am to judge others automatically I am judging myself.' - From Paula Tooths' #mymantratoday

9 – HOMŌ SŌLITARIUS

- Named after the Greek philosophers from the first millennium before Christ, was after 'Diogenes, the Cynic' die on the Corinth when the card had been spread between the readers. Contradictory as Hercules, his life model, the hero was cosmopolitan but commonly criticizes the values of corruption from his society.

- This card represents the deep search of the self. The person must retreat out of his zone of comfort and ambient to learn his lesson of wisdom. His unexpected step, makes the ones around misunderstand and judge inappropriate by his decisions.

- Sometimes called the master of shamanism leader, his experience doesn't show as a religious link. Brave and wise, this lamina isn't for everyone. Need the courage to gain the peace with the mind. After contemplating and meditate,

Homo Solitarius can bring light to the others so they may see better the next yard. Reclusion and the solitude is how he feeds his needs.

- Keywords for this trump are silence, guidance, inner power, retreat, reflection and introspection. Alchemy can be reminded as well, but not as a magic wise way. The card also can be interpreted as the old man who guides or a light of the world, or the time itself, which cures and make any fact or situation understandable.

- In aromatherapy, Frankincense and Cypress can shine the decisions and bless the spiritual retreat. For diet and nutrition, recommending the use of lime and drinking more water to make quicker the understanding of ones self.

- From Dr. Bach list, Crap Apple Flower Remedy could help the Homos Solitarius path, providing the cleansing and purification of his system.

Homo Solitaries Mantra: 'I am at peace with the world. My prosperity follows me when I follow my needs and desires.' - From Paula Tooths' #mymantratoday

10 – ROTA FORTŪNAE

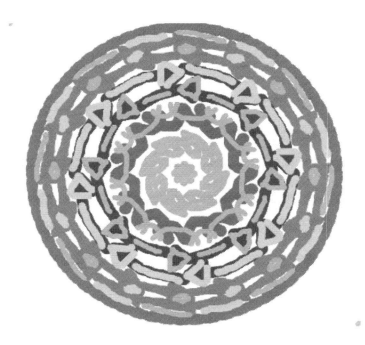

- This card is highly symbolic and to me it is the most important on the set. Mixed with inspiration, brings the blend of strength of old alchemy as salt, water, sulphur and mercury; Attach the angels on the clockwise movement but the serpents on the anti-clock maneuver. The division of eight spots turns on the idea of radiance and success. Rota Fortunae is basically the wheel from the Roman Goddess Fortuna, who used to make distribution of material and spiritual blessings, also meaning astrologically the point in the sky when the sun and moon are in the same line.

- Rota Fortunae shows a change in the fortune, what is good to remember that fortune and lucky do have different meanings. It symbolizes the ever-changing cycle of life, wins and losses, ups and downs, unexpected luck, advancements and setbacks, success and failure - the duality of things.

- Revealing a greater strength to work within, and learning from mistakes realized in the past, and what we have to learn with them; other keywords for this trump are success, victory, new beginnings, adaptation, chance, opportunities, elevation and fate.

- The diet calls attention for adding the critics recipes to revitalize the personal energy; and aromatherapy will point to a blend of rosemary, hyssop and clove in hazelnut oils to revitalize the good opportunities.

- The interesting pick on Dr. Bach Flowers Remedy list is Mustard, which will help to cope with the ups and downs of life as much as avoid or minimize depression, as much as disappear the lack of hope.

Rota Fortunae Mantra: 'I am ready to the new beginnings that appear in my life. If I commit a mistake or fail, I will be ready to start again and succeed with success.' - From Paula Tooths' #mymantratoday

11 – VĪRĒS

- Vires was originated after Heracles, Gatekeeper of Olympus and Patron of heroes, health and sports. Heracles was also the God of the oracles and the inspiration, well known as divine protector of their mythological world.

- This card has great inner strength and can face any challenge without being knocked down. The strength is also physical. Demonstrates a patience profile and natural leadership, holds a soft control because has a very persuasive personality. Full of tolerance and beauty, it's evolved in maternal skills and sportive abilities. Always compassionate for the task that he has in hands.

- Fortitude is a perfect measure between the flash and the love and it is directly represented with the heart and its chakra in Kundalini yoga.

- Perseverant, moderated, solid but kindness and disciplined, other words which can be used to translate this trump are control, composure, stability, efforts and inner strength.

- Adding Cardamom in the diet is highly recommended to bless the inner strength and Aromatherapy lineages advise the fortifying rosemary with thyme and the uplifting of blend counting on clary sage.

- The best choice of Dr. Bach Flower Remedies will be Wild Oat. That flower will magically make a connection of the strength with life measures and purposes.

Vires Mantra: 'I have a gallant spirit and I can manage any situation. I discard the fear because I hold the facts with love.' - From Paula Tooths' #mymantratoday

12 -- HŌMO SUSPENSUS

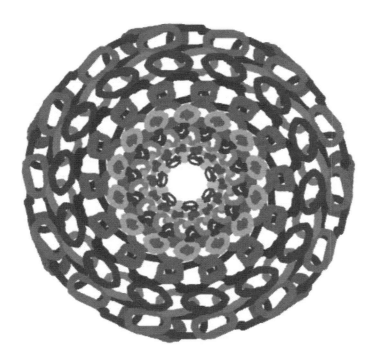

- Homo Suspensus card has the inspiration back to the Greek Titans - Prometheus, immortal who created the man from clay and still fire from the earth, was a very intellectual hero who established animal sacrifices, but had been punished from Zeus with eternal torment. The fore thinker become a symbol of theft and generally didn't make true the words he prays. The sun of light emerged in the darkness to conquer the self-interests selfishly. Other symbols related to it are tradition and a man who hangs himself because he cannot cope with his mistakes and faults.

- This lamina represents an adaptation for a new point of view; letting go of the past and surrendering to a situation. The new life shows the importance to be more vulnerable and flexibility, with an open mind. Good time to pause and reflect to realize what really is worth following. Maybe it's a sign that its time for renounces and put others' peoples interests first.

- Keywords for this card are altruism, suspension, loss, giving up, sacrifice, renunciation, nursing, acceptance, submission; it's a sort of person or situation that's always in between, holds doubt and for those facts, action doesn't flow naturally. But it makes us wonder massive questions and it probably is the main reason which keeps the traitor to your 'self' - are you prepared to give up to meet your goals?

- Attention at this point - its urgent a review of your diet! The seaweed kelp is advised to complete the diet of those figures and the best pick of aromatherapy will be myrrh and spikenard, what can be in notes of your perfumes or in the house fragrances, candles or bath creams.

- Using a blend made of Agrimony and Gentian from Dr. Edward Bach Flowers Remedy list, the Homo Suspensus will be able to leave the hanger from the tree.

Homo Suspensus Mantra: 'I let go of all judgments and life will bring me in a flow of truer relationships with the world at large.' - From Paula Tooths' #mymantratoday

13 – MORS

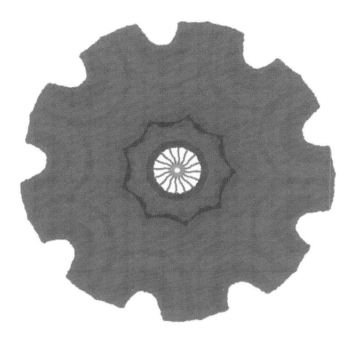

- Mors was inspired in the 'Divine Comedy', Dante mentions with a piece of dark wood in hands, the apocalypse as a dark night of the soul, the death of that act, to start a fresh new one. In that particular case, reputation was put in frame, when the majority couldn't understand the joke.

- Ending of a cycle and psychological transformation are the main means of this card. This conclusion can come followed by sadness and loss, but not necessarily Mors is the bad figure. So many situations can 'die' to give an open door to a good one; as the personal transformation can be to better. So many people have a personal awaken caused by a bad experience and 'killing' this situation to start with creates a brand new 'myself'. This card is sometimes hard to interpret and it's interesting how it can be 'good or bad', it will depend how you will workout and cope with the facts.

- The key word for this trump is change, finishing and restarting. Self-awareness and abort the old patterns, as much as work with the traumas left on you it is important when this draw appears.

- To work with aromatherapy, Chamomile could help to bring back the calm and the peace, Sandalwood to psycho and spiritual healing and Cedar to protection on the delicate situations. The diet is asking to be careful when trying to compensate feeling with carbohydrates and important is also adding of thyme

- As always-mentioned Dr. Edward Bach, changes aren't an easy path to follow, and to protect your thoughts at this point; the recommendation is to use a blend of Walnut Flower Remedy.

Mors Mantra: 'My mind is very strong and it is my everything. Wherever I think, I became. I am ready to go to the good changes I choose.' – From Paula Tooths' #mymantratoday

14 – TEMPERANTIA

- Inspired in Mayet, an old Egyptian Goddess who was responsible for the weather and the stars, regulates the truth and the justice; she had the task to make the decisions of the souls, if a creature was going to see the heaven or it will burn in the fire of the hell. The Goddess also is the model rule to the divinations and regulates the oracles, as the intermediate of the god of the gods as tells the mythology, she always will keep the world out of the chaos.

- The moderation of actions is required in this moment says this card. Holding the whole temperance of the world, the angel of this mandala has the power of unification and brings opposites together. Very moderated figure, it's a leader when the question is to reunite forces or join new ones.

- Transcendent is the Temperantia who will always blend people or situations, which in the past we couldn't even believe as a possibility. The ego is very high and sometimes we can take this slot as unconscious posture. Serene, is able to bring the feeling of security around. Consider other keywords as healing, health, harmony and balance.

- For health, Echinacea tinctures and blends are highly recommended as much as adding basil in the kitchen. To change the air and guarantee all this balance for Teperantia, chamomile tea is ideal. I must advise aromatherapies as angelica and bergamot.

- In Flowers Medicine, I would temper Honeysuckle, Willow and Scleranthus to create the maturity enough to keep the natural balance and generate the best decisions.

Temperantia Mantra: 'I am tuned into the divine universal wisdom and always understand the true meaning of life situations.' – From Paula Tooths' #mymantratoday

15 – DIABOLUS

- Back in the days when it didn't exist commercial printing and bibles were handmade, it qualified as a devil wherever a person who contradictories the summit of the biggest power who was concentrated in with the church or que person who put in question what those people are telling to be the unique truth. Holding this information in the corner of our minds, also in those days where we have not so much evidences of, the future tellers used their own decks of handmade drawn which after had been copied and spread. In some point, the card number 15 was lost. Its very hard to track what the original trump was but by long researches we can assume it was a figure of strength, persuasive, opinion maker, premature but didn't keep with his soul the best intentions with not to make himself happy. The card 15 needed to be replaced and as 'pagans'

TOOTHS / MANDALA LIFE COACH

the readers of those age created the devil figure instead. Sometimes related to the devil-god Apepi who in the old Egypt, in his snake form of life, let the sun god escape.

- Diabolus is the shadow. The part of us, which we hide for some or any reason. It represents our repressed feelings or what of us we mask because we ashamed of, not necessarily because its bad. This card can be interpreted as some in that holds us to grow. Sometimes, it can be seen as a grid portion or ambitious thoughts. This figure can be very aggressive if doesn't get its goals. Lies, discussions and illegal items can be awareness here.

- This card demonstrates with ignorance a selfish but passionate person. Beautiful, full of life and sexuality, the Diabolus knows exactly about the temptation we can fall for, and will try to seduce along this journey. It is the trump for the lust, obsessive relationships and physical attractions. Other keywords are: materialism, egoistic, pessimism, doubt, futility, passion, anxiety and anger. Other facts that can be attributed are addiction, depression and dependency.

- Patchouli will be the best pick of the essential oils in aromatherapy sciences and can use in many ways. The kitchen is desperate for the Cayenne pepper to give equilibrium to this strength.

- A blend of Sweet Chestnut and Impatiens probably will be the choice of Dr. Edward Back Flowers Remedy list with the goal to open boundaries and expand limits, to bring the best calm and understanding, balancing of this figure.

Diabolus Mantra: 'I am a light warrior. I choose love and happiness into my life because I'm guided by the truth.' – From Paula Tooths' #mymantratoday

16 – DOMUS DEI

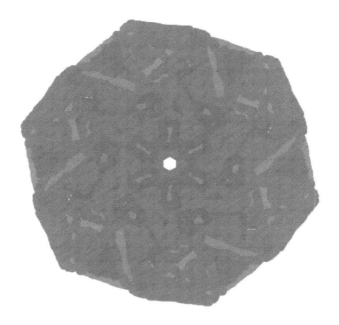

- This draw has been inspired on the Lord's house, where the whole population have had run for after the apocalypse. The highest part of the architecture was a tower where any person could reach the heaven, but usually the very top crumbles by their egos frustrations. Time to transcend. Deep meditation into yourself to realize a better way to see the world out of your pre-determined expectations.

- Time to re-evaluate and find space to the needed changes, this cards represents the fear of the unknown. It encourages coping with the emotional transformations and material loss. Generally it is the moment after a catastrophe when appears the uncertainty for the next step. We could call it a card of the broken heart. It is a request of existence to the one be strong and leave the bad experiences behind and enjoy the good ones to reconstruct a new moment.

- Lightening will come directly to the head after the paradigms created by the ego. Frustration can't be avoided. Keywords for this trump are crash, blow, disillusion and revelation; Impact, chaos and drama. It's interesting what this card bring up – your world will just fall down depending on your views of life, your expectations and the topics which you really believe in.

- Garlic is a recipe each can appear more into Domus Dei culinary. In aromatherapy, Pine is a good choice to play with.

- To find some peace and comfort, I would recommend the use of a blend with Oak and Star of Bethlehem from Dr. Bach Flowers Remedy list.

Domus Dei Mantra: 'I Release all fears and sorrow. I am exactly where I need to be. Now, with love, I embrace life.'– From Paula Tooths' #mymantratoday

17 – STĒLLA

- Inspirited in Urania, the muse of astronomy who often holds in hand an astrolabe, this card brings the literal meaning of this science toll etymology: stars taker. Commonly, this card is associated to Melusine, the twin tailed mermaid who is symbol of alchemy and many other times to the hero Aquarius, who historically has one foot fit in the floor and one into water.

- Stella is the trump of hope. After massive suffering and drastic changes, opportunities of a new portal will be shown and thinking positively, success will be achieved. Fresh inspiration and inner motivation magically will appear. This figure is generous and serene, but excessive peace of mind that can be sometimes flying away and this state confuses everybody around.

- This card can be understood as a navigator, pointing to the right direction. It's a blessed moment of discovery. Free flowing but free will is reminded. Key words for Stella are optimism, joy, faith, tranquility, peace, and trust and renew/ regeneration.

- To provoke relaxation, blends with Chamomile can cause very interesting effects. The use of extra lime and lemon in the meals can awake the answers to find the right ways to follow. In aromatherapy, eucalyptus can assure the faith and help your unconscious to re-discovery the self.

- Restoring the hope and confidence, a good mix of Dr. Bach Flower Remedies is Elm and Gorse. It will put the faith in track and make your more deep desires believes that everything is possible. Miracles happen all the time!

Stella Mantra: 'My inner star shines and guides me in good direction. Success follows me wherever where I am.' - From Paula Tooths' #mymantratoday

18 – LŪNA

- Luna was created with inspiration in the map of the Universe and the shadows that the moon makes to hide every single space of the earth or the parts of the water. The moon covers the light but as it moves creates a new opportunity so light can shine again.

- Card of fertilization, Very attractive, full of self light, this figure causes lots of doubts and missing the clarity, the imagination will be activated to evolve your thoughts in fantasy. Confused, the anxiety of the environment will bring up new worries and fears of the mysteries of life.

- This trump represents the conflict between our dreams and nightmares, losing direction and clarity; reflecting a hard emotional period. Other key words for this card are uncertainty, tension, phobias, distortions, and inner demons.

- This figure is asking some marjoram to be added in your meals. In aromatherapy, sandalwood can be used in the body and in the house. Like a magic potion it can help to open the paths.

- Honeysuckle and Rock Rose must be the choice. This blend made from Bach Flower Remedies will be to keep the person in track and to motivate the courage forgotten.

Luna Mantra: 'I release the chains of fear and now I can see clear. I am open to new opportunities.'- From Paula Tooths' #mymantratoday

19 – SŌL

- Handsome and very strong, the best leader in combat and full of magical powerful objects and a horse called Lugh, the Sun God in the old Celtic Mythology and was after him that this card was drawn. Bright, strong hands and long arms were the remarkable characteristics of this personage of History but it was with his harp that he still smiles in everybody's hearts.

- Innocent to a certain point, Sol represents strength in life, enthusiasm for the new starts. Motivated, this figure can win any battle. Sometimes temper, but it shows that at any time the best moment is always the 'now'. Always renewing, rediscovery about him/herself everyday and brings a fresh hope to any future. Invigorating moments are to appear because Sol understood the sun appears to

TOOTHS / MANDALA LIFE COACH

all and has the certainty that all is possible when you really are committed to do something.

- Phoenix personality, this card shows a multi-tasked person, full of talents, really optimistic, who is always open to learn about any subject and gain spiritual skills on a daily basis because they are always is looking for it. We would say that it is a sort of person who has a self-light, with much personal power. Key words for this trump are vitality, reality, shine, victory, expansion, confidence, assurance and positivism.

- Olive Flower Remedy is very recommended with this card and for the reversal case, when appears the lack of energy, I would prescribe Rescue Blend from Dr. Edward Bach.

Sol Mantra: 'I can do anything I want to because I trust my thoughts. I release procrastination and full of enthusiasm I work on my goals now.' - From Paula Tooths' #mymantratoday

20 – IŪDICIUM

- Inspired by the Angel from the judgment day - probably Archangel Raphael, this card clearly reminds us of the opportunity to rest the past and surrender ourselves to the present; that forgiven is our basic need. The announcement to the soul of the acceptance of the self. After all, sins are spit out and buried. The innocence reflecting this angel allows us to command our existence, which is reborn and again is free to be.

- This Mandala represents the fire, which burns the past and with it comes the new beginnings. All is forgotten and forgiven and the remade self understands the lesson presented. The figure is healed and has renewed vows, ready to the great transformation.

- It's the card of causes and effects, which means letting go. A door is closed in some point but a massive gate will be open if the experience is absorbed. The paradise life promised as compensation is ready to arrive now. Key words in this read are decision, acceptance, hope, release, resurrection, redemption, reconciliation, forgiveness, judgment and inner call.

- Anise tea is excellent to clean and heal the soul. In aromatherapy, the healing properties of Lavender can clean and purify the energy of the fields. Use and abuse of this aroma!

Iudicium Mantra: 'When I forgive others, I forgive myself. I find rebirth into my actions to find the best possible results.' - From Paula Tooths' #mymantratoday

21 – MUNDUS

- Mundus lamina is inspired in the Universe itself and the five related elements. Water meaning the wisdom, Air meaning the feelings and emotions, Fire meaning the strength, Earth meaning the background and Aether meaning the spirit. It also comes back to the belief that all is one and the end can become the start. Basically, it is these that we just made from energy and we are an integration of all the senses and experiences possible.

- Radiant, a quite materialistic, this cards represents the time to personal grown, that learn to share and contribute to the out world an immediately is compensated with happiness. This is the moment to learn that love is giving; receiving it's a consequence.

- This is the Mandala that shows colours in your visions, dreams coming true. Restored feelings and a fresh brand new life are ahead. The figure finally – after really hard work – and complete all the tasks and missions, manage to reach the full success. Other key words can relay in this trump are wholeness, prosperity, achievement, satisfaction, compliment, success and integration.

- Herbalism shows up with Hibiscus, which healing powers will bring back feelings, underline the wisdom, clean the blockages and energize the wishes. In other hand, aromatherapy advices passionflower and apple scent notes to give a total equilibrium between the material and abstract; body and soul.

- On Dr. Bach's sciences, the best picks to have the vision of the lesson in the experiences and to gain strength and follow well the next duties are Chestnut Bud and Hornbean Flower Remedies.

Mundus Mantra: 'I am conscious of my wholeness. I have found my place in this world; there is so much more I can do and can experience.' – From Paula Tooths' #mymantratoday

22 – SCURRA

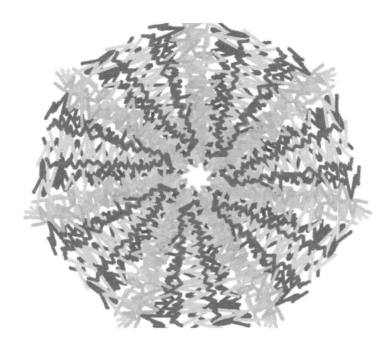

- Inspired on the old jesters, who after originated from the English Royal licensed fools, then the Shakespearean literature fools and after had the playing cards 'joker' named after them. Jesters appear really early in history, who were usually males hired to entertain the high court for a little amount of money coins or just for food. Those celebrities were intellectual high profile people who convert their brains into jokes to make the royalty laugh in very private shows. The professional Buffoons as they were called, are people who managed to make fun of themselves or make fun of politics and respectable people well known on their time and community.

- Remembering that in this first group one trump it's follow scenery to the previous fact as we saw it in a circle, this card can induce the mind to complete the meaning of any other card, as being any card else. Full of knowledge as not much recognized or compensated, Scurra grabs the exuberant teen years hunger of life, doubts, dreams and fights for beliefs that later realize isn't exactly what was the meaning. This figure can be the protagonist of a history or can be hidden with the mysteries of a mind. It's their unlimited potential and so many skills to show. This Mandala is an open mind of those who are never tired to learn.

- With sensitive and unprotected life, the Scurra can mean a person in the discovery of the way of divination, and risks taken above the fears on the path of unknown subjects. It may also be a warning that significant change is coming. This card can be related to other key words as faith, spontaneous, beginnings, simplicity, innocence, individuality, free spirit, and free will, adventurous, seeker of life, excitement and risk.

- The kitchen asks for adding ginseng to reboot the cosmic energy, as fennel drinks are really welcome as well. Aromatherapy advises niaouli essential oils as much as lotus aroma notes in uncountable sources, to reassure the potential, keep the balance and promote an encounter with the self-light.

- Dr. Edward Bach flower medicine list will point to an interesting mix of Aspen and Chicory Remedies.

Scurra Mantra: 'I am gifted. I just give space to positive feelings. I use my all my resources and willpower to achieve my goals. I make all beginnings all the time I need to.' – From Paula Tooths' #mymantratoday

GROUP 2 – GEOMETRIA

"Excellence is never an accident. It is always the result of high intention, sincere effort, and intelligent execution; it represents the wise choice of many alternatives - choice, not chance, and determines your destiny." — Aristotle

23 – UNUS

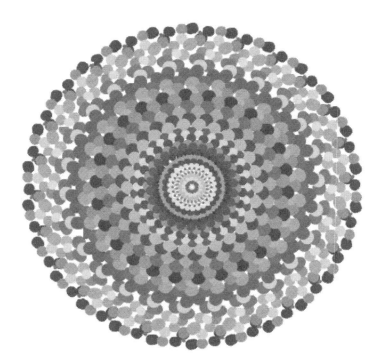

- This second group, geometry is based in math's and numerology sciences. Inspired by the main key of numbers, Unus will represent the number one. A powerful force that produces results and does not allow anything or anyone to limit its potential.

- This card represents beginnings, the start of the seasons. Aggressive figure, which will bring up the necessary energy to produce and achieve it goals. Hard worker but not workaholic, pioneirist and a natural born leader. Full of determination, the motivation here comes from the focus and determination.

- Independent and self critical, finds difficulty in being a follower and answering other's expectations. Very sociable, this figure knows very well how to express it's self. Keywords are deep, jovial, friendly, positive, adventurous, kindness and power.

- Kitchen is desperate for spinach and bay leaves are highly recommended as much all the grease should be avoided, to keep going as the strongest. In aromatherapy, grapefruit will keep you inner power always up.

- To follow with integrity, with control of your past experiences and motivation enough to re-start, I would recommend a mix of Cherry Plum, Hornbean and Chestnut Bud from Dr. Bach Flowers Essences.

Unus Mantra: 'I show others a good example as an inspirational leader. Every day in every way I am improving all my capacities.' – From Paula Tooths' #mymantratoday

24 – DUO

- Inspired in the united, equilibrium, and universal symmetry, Duo is the number which always comes in pairs; in the material world in the twin way and psychological issues, this number will always been related with feelings in reciprocity. There is the balance, union, relationships and co-operation.

- Patient, brilliant listener, friendly and unpretentious, Duo usually represents a female figure very strong and with so many times full of power or able enough to retain it, but most of the situations wont find recognition of her actions. Full of beauty and musicality, diplomacy and dreams, it is very spiritually influenced and likes a modest life. Devotion to truth and simplicity is of major importance. The hidden abilities always appear as a good surprise to the Universe.

- Owner of natural gentleness, always passive, very understanding and forgiving, Duo is brilliant to work into a tem and very obey when it's needed. Its also uncomplicated and stable, what makes this trump very easy going is her (his) path to be sure that the person around will always shine. The keywords Generosity, serenity, sociability, cordiality, kindness, affection, loyalty, romance and enthusiasm.

- This card personal and professional environment will be lots happier with some colourful roses. It will make the view more interesting and the perfume will ascend the power beneath its adjectives. Chamomile integrated in the meals and as drinks can bring massive benefits.

- To exercise the patience and the diplomacy, deal with personal/ affective needs and underline the power and abilities hidden; the best pick will be a blend of Impatiens, Beech and Heather from Dr. Bach Flowers medicine list.

Duo Mantra: 'I feel balanced and patient. I radiate love and happiness. Me, my thoughts, my wishes and the Universe are in line.' – From Paula Tooths' #mymantratoday

- Inspired by the Holy Trinity – The Father, the son and the Holy Ghost; it's a card which brings immediately the idea of creation of all. Taking 'religion' away and put in to modern words I would say that Unus was the father, Duo was the mother and now Tres, comes as a talented child.

- Masculine, creative, innovator and talk-active, its very political. Naturally spoiled and has an ability to bring around light to the Universe, to brighten up the thought from the ones who insist to live in the darkness. Rhythm always will be the sense of their lives, not if just the heart beats or the noise from the rain.

- Very intelligent academically and spiritual, prone to find in this trumps teachers, mentors and gurus. Sociable, adaptable and versatile are probably other keywords that more often will appear with this trump. Discipline can be a problem, but time can be a good teacher. Luck follows the Tres everywhere.

- Using the focus to unleash the creativity and absorb the negatives, find frankincense and rosemary for the body and the spaces. For the kitchen, including the drinks, the good picks are nutmegs and cinnamon.
- To live this life intensely, make the right decisions and enjoy the opportunities, I would recommend Scleranthus, and to add some spiritual and energetic protection added to the motivation to concretize dreams – Clematis and Walnut from Dr. Bach Essences list.

Tres Mantra: 'I am like fire that shines and water that flows; the earth that supports and air that cleans. I am the teacher and my best student is myself. My illuminated thoughts bring creative solutions.' – From Paula Tooths' #mymantratoday

26 - QUATTUOR

- Inspired in the history of geometrical, Quattuor is a number with the biggest meaning. Magical geometry is based in the number four, as much here it is related to the stable of life as: 4 seasons, 4 faces of a cube, 4 corners of a space/ building magic's; the 4 directions and 4 basic elements of earth.

- This cards brings a figure really good with organization and cleaning; good skills about management and very hard worker but is always expecting the results to come with no-efforts. Always will compensate itself and others in a material way.

- This card shows efficiency, productivity, realism, and stability. Concentration is vital for the system and security permanently a goal. Other keywords for this trump are helpful, trustful, practicality and lack of direction.

- Quattuor can grab the feet into earth and feel all the natural strength as aromatherapy advises Cypress, bergamot and geranium. Using all together, this card never more will feel lack of direction or security!

- To look after the health and never be tired again; and find courage to move forward, I would recommend a blend of Mimulus and Olive from Dr. Edward Bach Remedies. Rock water could help with the perfectionist personality knocks.

Quattuor Mantra: 'I am stable and secure. I am living my achievement because I choose the right direction instead the velocity. I am wealthy now.' – from Paula Tooths' #mymantratoday

- Inspired on the new age mystical prime number, five usually comes represented by a star, also called 'the pentagram'. The five points of the pentagram, this means the quintessential (or spirit) pointing to the top, followed by the four elements – air (on the top left), earth (bottom left), fire (bottom right) and water (on the top right) back to the spirit, demonstrating that life is a cycle. Keeping the idea of constantly looping, this star brings the idea of a creation of human-being and the projection of human's five ends – the head pointed up and the four main limbs, considering the man, or human, open to the world as a cross. With the human figure, it can be noted the five continuously – are there 5 fingers/toes, 5 senses (sight, hearing, smell, touch and taste), 5 stages of life (birth, adolescence, coitus, parenthood and death) and 5 virtues (generosity, courtesy, chastity, chivalry and piety).

- Freedom is the big mystery to be reached, becoming sometimes a lifetime challenge. This card represents the new. New changes, new choices, new opportunities, new life. Full of innovative and imaginative ideas, it's very adventurous and always will find a way to travel and see new places and meet different people. Impatient and Impulsive, it can find there's a trouble with discipline and organization. Never settles if it does not learnt the lesson of freedom.

- Very comfortable in front of big audiences, Inspiring and motivator, naturally able to change how people think. On the other hand, this trump shows a very sensuous person, who also is very difficult to fit in a relationship, but very faithful. Other keywords are ambitious, progressive, bright-minded, adaptable, inquiring, exploring, and promoting and independence.

- To heal the challenges and promote the peace and balance within this Mandala is recommended scents as vetiver and myrrh.

- Dr. Edward Bach best pick will be a blend of Walnut, Impatiens and Scleranthus Flower Remedies to help to deal with the choices, calm the energy and general direction.

Quinque Mantra: 'I am free to be myself. I effectively manage my life. My path is filled with amazing opportunities.' – From Paula Tooths' #mymantratoday

28 - SEXh

- Inspired in the six days of creation and the six attributes of the creator - power, wisdom, majesty, love, mercy and justice, also in the Star of David and its double triangle representing the balance between the men and the divine; and the fusion creating equilibrium between male and female; positive and negative; and of course the Hindu divine Trinity which brings back to the creation with the union of the 3 Gods – Brahma, Vishnu and Shiva. Scientists believe that the hexagram is a very ancient symbol but the most powerful.

- Sexh represents the union, the perfection, and ideal existence. It's very simple and domestic, tolerant, laid back and very giving. This figure will never be selfish and so sharing that take from self to give to others. Cheerful, seeker of life and new joys, always committed to goals and proposes.

- This card isn't attached to the material world, doesn't give value to money or success. All is deep – the love, the feelings, honesty and faith. Very humanitarian, make life just a courier to look after everybody else interests and happiness. Other keywords are responsibility, orientation, direction, balance, focus, discipline, love, relationships, generosity, kindness, care, and happiness. It's a "mother" trump.

- Aromatherapy advises for this Mandala sandalwood and lemongrass, relaxing and opening the mind to new horizons. Adding basil in sorted ways in the kitchen will bring extra focus and its great for clarity and give a new history to the productivity in daily basis.

- Red Chestnut Flower Remedy can help with the over worries with others and Vervain can aid in dealing to look after the self instead the others. Using these two essences from Bach list will help to find the complete balance.

Sexh Mantra: 'I love who I have become. I recognize the many good qualities I have. I am welcoming all changes that come into my life now.'– From Paula Tooths' #mymantratoday

- Inspired in the seven pillars of wisdom, in the seven stars composing the Big Dipper equally the seven stars of the Little-Dipper constellation and the seven chakras. Septem is the number of alchemists, and eternal symbol of occult.

- This card represents the spirituality, wisdom and mystery. The intuition that can develop the motivation and strength to uncover the unknown. Because it is a 'gifted' figure usually appears alone, studying, researching or seeking for answers. Very intellectual, but introspective. Often doesn't know how to share the hidden knowledge. It can lightly symbolize our internal struggles.

- Exotic and individualist, qualified as cold, distance and particular dry trump. Its not related to material aspects. Original, Hard worker and doesn't mind how much or if will receive any compensation for that and doesn't need supervision.

Septem aren't sociable at all, always will choose the adventure into a book instead a friends meeting or a party. Always under flexibility, other keywords that this Mandala carries are analyst, bright, eccentric, curious, technical, inventive, meditation, oneness, charismatic, solitude, peace, religious, perfectionist.

- Apple and cucumber are recommended as much as fruit juices to regulate the health and intelligence. In aromatherapy, notes of Jasmine, Lavender and Frankincense are advised to awaken the mystical inside, to shine the intellectual powers and social integrates.
- Walnut, Water Violet and Agrimony Flower Remedies from Dr. Bach list are very recommended within this card to deal with loneliness and finding energetic protection.

Septem Mantra: 'Life excites me. I am expressing love toward myself and all others today. I now work to improve my total being.' – From Paula Tooths' #mymantratoday

30 - OCTO

- Inspired in an eight number flipped on its side is an infinity symbol and within the Wheel of the Year, there are eight Sabbaths typically observed by Wiccans and many Pagans, often represented with the eight solstices and equinoxes, symmetric shared in an eight pointed star; meaning a year events calendar.

- Octo lamina represents the universal spiritual law of causes and effects. This figure is authority, wealth and very successful. The card is related to political talent, involving lots of persuasion. It's a very decisive position but rounded with judgment.

- Executive appearance, it's a number of material matters. If linked to a human being, can mean a very successful business prosperous, talented, family oriented and protective. Everything that you do has repercussions. It comes back to you one way or another. So, It's time to watch the way you live your life because you reap what you sow Spiritual conscious and responsible, other keywords reading this trump are realism, management, wisdom, status and stability, truth, confident, ambitious, authoritarian, self-confident, integrity, challenge, efficiency, trustworthy and abundance.

- Hibiscus teas or drinks and aromatherapy based in lotus essential oils may influence the deeper understanding of the self beyond the physical or material. A blend with notes of Frankincense, Benzoin, Myrrh and Cedarwood can help to find the connection with Universe and the spiritual meaning of life.

- Using Dr. Edward Bach Flower essences list, Elm could have an important paper helping to deal with this material abundance. In order to do not lose material and emotional control, a blend of Cherry Plum and Holly can be very useful.

Octo Mantra: 'I believe in infinite abundance and the money is always there. Each day I live in the moment, by forgiving those in my past.'– From Paula Tooths' #mymantratoday

- Inspired in the nine months of gestation of human being, Novem is a card which shows the creation of the universe through the birth as believes the Tantric Yantra Dowsing as well. We could easily remember here the re-birth via the nine gates to the hell or sometimes called nine cycles. Also, nine is the magic number in the Mayan civilization and probably the biggest influence come from the Nine muses of Greek mythology – the 9 daughters of Zeus are Goddess art patrons - Calliope (epic poetry and eloquence), Euterpe (music and lyric poetry), Erato (love poetry), Polyhymnia (oratory or sacred poetry), Clio (history), Melpomene (tragedy), Thalia (comedy), Terpsichore (choral song and dance), and Urania (Astronomy).
- This Mandala is an achiever, thinker with massive problems solving capabilities.

  This figure is experienced and can see facts in a big picture, easily finding best

  solutions. It's because this figure is a sincere friend, if something is done against

  him, take some time or forever to they let it go. As the Mayans mention, it is a very high profile person or situation, yet holds all the characteristics from all the previous numbers.

- Light workers, has compassion for others and is a natural leader who the most of the time they have a hidden artistic talent. Investors, they write big goals and go for it, costs what costs they don't give up. The big pleasure here is to be the centre of all attentions. This card has the need to learn to live in the present and let go the past. Other keywords can find related to this trump are humanitarianism, charity, magnetism, purpose, creative, sensitive, loyal, eccentricity, communicative, influential, and perfection.

- Aromatherapy highly recommends scents of violet leafs and Fredonia. These notes will help to meditate and bring up old issues and making easy to solve them. Phytotherapy call the ancient origins of the "Nine Herbs", also well known as Old English Charms. But we don't need go this far in literature. Adding some fennel, thyme and chamomile to meals and drinks can be very useful with this trump.

- Honeysuckle and Walnut Flower Remedies are the best indications from Dr. Bach list; helping to release the past, deal with losses and training the unconditional love with the self, which doesn't need other probation.

Novem Mantra: 'I joyfully release all of the past and let only love surround me. Now, I focus my power in the present and I change my life.' – From Paula Tooths' #mymantratoday

32 – UNDECIM

- In Chemistry, the 'group 11' contains the noble metals: copper, silver and gold, but it isn't the unique inspiration. Tracing back in history, we mention here already the Star of David (five-pointed star) and the Seal of Salomon (six-pointed star). Opposing one to another gave us the Unicursal Hexagram. The symbol as a whole makes eleven; five petals of the rose and six vertices of the hexagram. As the cabalistic tree of life counts with eleven petals meaning the same number of steps of mastering. Eleven is the first master number.

- Spiritual coach, Undecim symbolizes the potential to push the limitations of the human experience into the stratosphere of the highest spiritual perception; the link between the mortal and the immortal; between man and spirit; between darkness and light; ignorance and enlightenment. It's the balance between the positive and the negative.

- This Mandala is a spiritual channel and also an educator. It's instinctive; highly evolved with religions and all related no non-material world. Other keywords linked to this card are illuminator, messenger, spiritual intuition, will, visionary, revelation, ritual, alchemy, sensitivity, humanitarianism, compassion and creativity.

- Echinacea tea will protect your energy and give an extra strength to your thoughts. To move to strike a new chord of inspiration and ambition in our lives, this trump may count with aromatherapy skills; Oakmoss, Blood Orange and cedar can just maybe open the portals 11:11 and make dreams come true.

- Picking a blend made with Agrimony, Walnut, Larch and Elm flower remedies from Dr. Bach list, would aid to track in the spiritual self-coaching.

Undecim Mantra: 'I am a source of love, hope and healing energy to every soul I encounter today. My spiritual progression path grows stronger with daily practice.' – From Paula Tooths' #mymantratoday

33 – VIGINTI DUO

- The inspiration here is divine. Twenty-two is the second master number. Are twenty-two the paths joined in the tree of life, are twenty two letters on the sacred Hebrew alphabet, are twenty two cards on the Major Arcana of the classic Tarot.

- This trump has similar abilities as the previous card added a rare talent of applying instinctive perception of the non-material realm to merely practical, grounded activities. It's the figure that is the high spiritual but can achieve the top material world simultaneously. World citizen, very persistent and doesn't see importance in borders or racial differences.

- Viginti Duo represents the big dreams. With this card appears a big challenge about inflating the ego but in other frames it's also a creator of clarity and

TOOTHS / MANDALA LIFE COACH

security. Very self-confident, this Mandala also is charged with other keywords such as discipline, leadership, idealism, pressure, practical, femininity and supremacy. This lamina, the self will be an eternal challenge.

- In the kitchen is highly recommended adding Ginger in the meals and drinks to aid with the spiritual comprehension of materialistic realm. Aromatherapy sciences advise powerful notes as Black Pepper, Bergamot and White Grapefruit to help to cope with nervous strain and to bring up the master spirit, which is hidden in the body.

- Oak, Impatiens, Pine and Verbena Flower Essences from Dr Bach studies used in a daily blend will manage to start a path to nirvana.

Viginti Duo Mantra: 'I am grateful for the daily opportunity Universe gives me to master others. I am thankful for the limitless overflowing source of my abundance. I give generously to myself and others.' – From Paula Tooths' #mymantratoday

GROUP 3 — ELEMENTOS

"The greatest mistake in the treatment of diseases is that there are physicians for the body and physicians for the soul, although the two cannot be separated." – Plato

34 – TERRAE

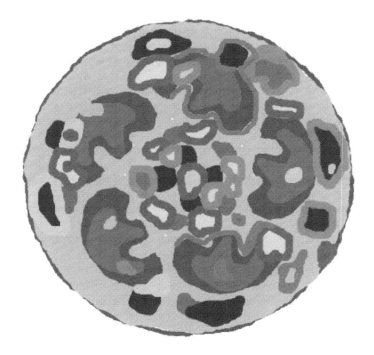

- Inspired on the element of Earth, in its natural beauty and the abundance of sources. It's the overview of different aspects of our expectations about the world that we live into. It's here where all the other elements take place together, providing a union. This draw in ancient studies can represent the physical body of the human being and the connection between the earth and our physical body.

- This card represents the beginning stage of some big dream but follow of success and prosperity, the endless opportunities that we can find in the present life, handful of history behind. This mandala is a perfect union of material, the physical and the sensual.

- Sometimes stubborn and a quite resistant to natural changes, carrying the challenge of adaptation. Very passive but things are grounded. Things are stable and sustain life. With solid fruitful foundation, other keywords related to this trump are solid, productive, practical, abundance, loyalty, commitment, substance, growth, patience, tolerance, slow, shape, stability, fragrance/ odour, determination and material wealth.

- In Ayurveda, this figure represents Dhra and is highly recommended adding banana in drinks and meals. To maintain a strong connection to life proposes and the stability in balance, aromatherapy sciences recommends notes of Ho leaf, Cedar wood, geranium and rosewood.

- For this Mandala, Holly Flower Remedy is the choice on Dr. Bach list to keep the round, help with focus and be worry less.

Terrae Mantra: 'I stand firmly in my life in a loving and imaginative way. I release all my fears and I very welcome abundance.' – From Paula Tooths' #mymantratoday

- Inspired in the element of Air, probably the mandala which is most related to Aquarius Era. Related to the chakra of the heart, it's the first basic need of life, responsible for all type of motion or movement. Understanding as well it as oxygen, it also is the basis for all energy transfer reactions.

- This trump is known as the Force of Thought. Aer is intellectual, communicators, logical, idealistic and objective. Auto coaching, its here where the self will find the internal school to learn how to think. The challenge is the speech that requires breath, which requires air.

- Vital for life, this Mandala is very cleansing but sometimes devastating. Can cause 'burn' if provoked. Very much active, intellectual and logical, other related key words are co-operative, truth, creative, reason, spiritual, school, inventive, unconditional love, self healing, joy, alert, sociable, clarity and justice.

- Using the Ayurveda Nutrition, this card represents Vayu and it loves all variety of beans. Roses in the house can help to persuade and be understood by others. Frankincense, Myrrh and Yarrow are the scents aromatherapy recommends for improve focus and mental clarity.

- Agrimony Flower Essence will be the best pick from Dr. Edward Bach sciences to keep Aer grounded and balanced.

Aer Mantra: 'I release now all the negative thoughts. I am open to giving and receiving love. I'm ready to share my knowledge.' – From Paula Tooths' #mymantratoday

36 – IGNIS

- Inspired in the element fire and the spiritual body that it represents, it's from the fire that we get the light and the hot, essentials on our paths. Fire is the energy that binds atoms together.

- Ignis is the card of the force of the spirit. This figure has energy, attitude, enthusiasm and motivation. Here is the house of passion, the lovers and relationships. This trump is a initiator of transformations and causes rejuvenation wherever what it touchs. Ignis also is associated to the passion to our 'self', our secret faiths and wisdom; when awake actives our psychic senses; that gives us courage of conviction and drives us towards fulfillment and wholeness.

- Powerful, this Mandala is full of confidence and courage. Leader, other keywords related to this trump are creativity, expression, desire, inspiring, initiates, leadership, enthusiastic, spontaneous, self-sufficient, romantic and ardent.

- In order to awake the powers of this drawn, I would go deep in aromatherapy and choose sharp notes of black pepper, ginger and orange essential oils. In the kitchen, I would recommend basil and ginger adding to meals and drinks. Impatiens flower remedy from Dr. Bach essences list may help to improve the calm to flow easily for the chosen goals and balance the energy.

Ignis Mantra: 'I move toward my goals. I am very motivated and I take the necessary actions because my dreams follow me.' – From Paula Tooths' #mymantratoday

37 – AQUA

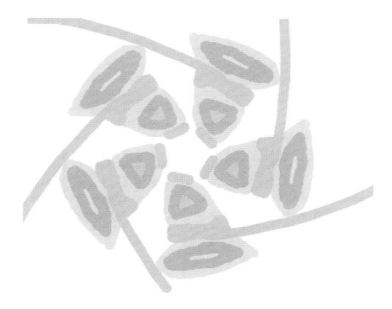

- Inspired on the element water, what also represents the blood, which circulates and moves our journeys. Water is very interesting – it holds the three absolute states – solids, liquids and gas; rise and falls; it's very flexible and its movement is part of this element. It's the most of our physical bodies, nourishes the planet, cleanses and reflects actions. If not well controlled, anything can happen to Aqua. Better look very careful to the feelings of your thoughts can shine up to you!

- Sensuous, this Mandala represents the feelings, the emotions and the intuition. It means the love in the prurient sense. It's emotional, sustaining, responsive and deep. Learning to go with the flow is especially difficult challenge for those who identify more readily with their ego, body, or mind.

- Healing, owner of wise intuition, reflect back the light of the truth. Force of emotions but realistic till a point, here we front very positive keywords: compassion, sensitivity, sexuality, psychic, artistic, intuitive, love, peace, purification and helpful.

- Aromatherapy will narrow to two essential oils Jasmine and Sandalwood that will help with the natural abilities. In the kitchen, adding lime and chamomile to meals and drinks may influence to balance the system.

- Dr. Bach Sciences will recommend a blend of Honeysuckle and Star of Bethlehem Flower Remedies to keep the path flowing well.

Aqua Mantra: 'I release all bad feeling and I open now the space to the true love instead. All of my thoughts and emotions flow harmoniously and my desires are perfectly balanced.' – From Paula Tooths' #mymantratoday

38 – AETHER

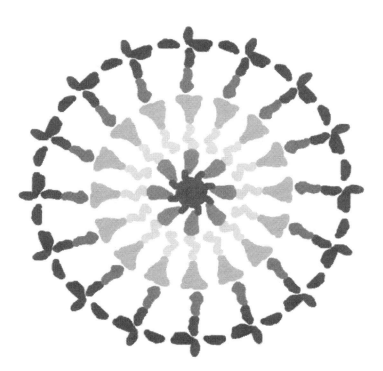

- Aether, sometimes called spits by alchemists and Wicca's, is the prime element present in all things, providing space, connection and balance for all Elements to exist. Aether is immaterial unlike the Air, Fire, Water and Earth. As principle of chemistry, we are made of Aether as well, in other words, we are all spirits. Vibrational healing presumes that we are made of energies. We are all connected in a cyclical interaction of generation and destruction, which balances life.

- This trump is described as the space where everything happens. All matter exists in space. Space is everywhere and touches everything. In our body, it is present in all cavities like nostrils, mouth, ears, throat, lungs, and stomach; as in blood vessels it receives all impressions. In heart, it accepts love. Aether is soft, light, subtle and abundant, provides space, looseness, open, sound and non-resistance. Grief will be the time life challenge.

- The order here is that the cycle of life is the eternity. This Mandala is essential to our sense of connectedness with spirit and well being. Aether represents the sense of joy and union. Higher receptive, other keywords that well represent this card are bliss, communication, self-expression, and truth

- Supporting our inner strength and fortitude with oils such as frankincense, rose, jasmine, rosewood, elemi, sandalwood, neroli and ylang ylang shows that aromatherapy can help. In the kitchen, tea tree and turmeric are useful to detox and learn to deal with receptivity and acceptance. Blueberries and all blue foods/ drinks are recommended as well to uplift the mysterious spiritual powers.

- The best pick on the Dr. Edward Bach Flower essences list is White Chestnut that can aid in restful sleep and guarantee sweet dreams.

Aether Mantra: 'I am whole and I am balanced. My soul is boundless and infinite. I trust that everything in my life has real purpose and always works out for the good of the Universe.' – From Paula Tooths' #mymantratoday

39 - METALLUM

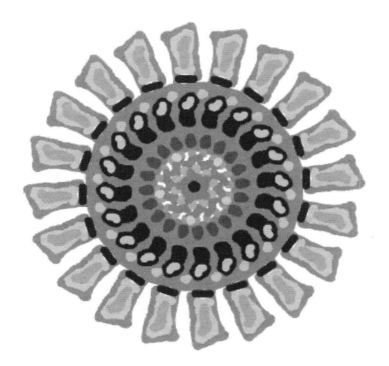

- Inspired in the element of metal from the traditional Chinese medicine. Diverging than the most people's thoughts, its physical expression as well as in mind and spirit and unexpected to the most, hands us many purposes.

- This Mandala doesn't deal well with extremes. Metallum is a figure who hides in the autumn and is always afraid of the imbalance of the hot and when life drops cold as well. It's in the nature that this card finds the harmony that the spirit as asking for. Extremely rigid and connected to this word, refinement and self-esteem are priority.

- Great integrity, remain unresponsive in relationships, but when requested stands with others around. Correct and fair, centred figure that doesn't give space to disorder and conflict. The strongest keywords with this trump are logical, methodical, efficient, perfection, structure and control.

- Silver fir will be the advice from aromatherapy to serve the aloofness and release the past. Lavender and eucalyptus scents will push back the balance to the whole structure. The diet is here begging for cardamom and cypress.

- Holly and Rock Water Flower Essences from Dr. Bach will be the best pick to help to deal with all sorts of love and to gain some flexibility.

Metallum mantra: 'I release my old patterns. I am strong and it makes me very flexible. My whole structure is balanced with love.' – From Paula Tooths' #mymantratoday

40 – LIGNUM

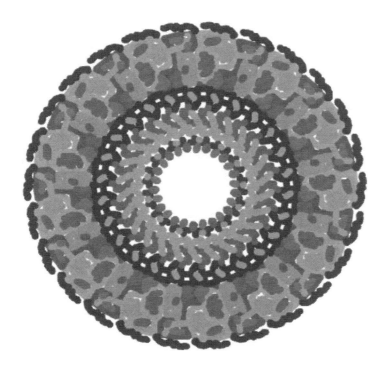

- The inspiration lays again on the traditional Chinese medicine. Wood is all about growth, change and expansion. Spring is when everything can happen.

- Very confident and motivated, this card has the ability to indicate the future and present insights for the best choices to go for it. Taking that easily can plan strategically the next steps. Lignum loves changes and challenges, works well with pressure and respects borders and time. This Mandala likes pretty much to take decisions but as a tree, it requests flexibility and abilities to dance life's melody.

- Alive and assertive, full of activity and resources, other key words linked to this trump are competiveness grown, background, routes, courage, still, ambitious, creation, implementation, grounding and strength.

- Aromatherapy can help in order to relieve emotions and restlessness related to thwarted expression: guilt, jealousy and anger; activates personal creativity and balances emotional and mental energy with single essential oils as roman chamomile, spike lavender, blue yarrow, spikenard, bergamot and grapefruit. Lime and lemon adding to meals and drinks will help to awake the hart and open the mind.

- Oak Flower Remedy can recall the soul purpose. But a mix of Beech, Impatiens, Rock Water, Vervain, Wild Rose Flower Essences, also from Dr. Bach list can help with a full balance of this card structure.

Lignum Mantra: 'I am in contact to my higher self. I am motivated to make changes and confident that all my plans are blooming every day.' – From Paula Tooths' #mymantratoday

GROUP 4 – FIORA MEDICINAE

"Treat the cause not the effect."

- Dr. Edward Bach

41 – AGRIMONIA

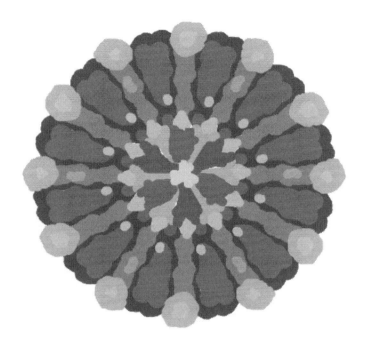

- Inspired in the plant of Agrimonia eupatoria (Rosaceae), which has yellow flowers blooming in July and August, on British summer. Roman folklore has evidences of the use of it on witchcraft, in particular to cure with wounds from riffles. Herbology believes this flower can improve situations of male impotence. Homeopathy uses species of Agrimonia to deal with indigestion, menstrual problems, kidneys difficulties, bladder and bronchorrhea.

- This mandala represents the emotional honest with oneself. Young, happy, enthusiastic, popular and seemingly at peace with the world at least in the appearance.

- This card remembers a brave face but very tormented with a multi active mind, difficulties to relax and meditate. Sometimes here we can front a lack of acceptance of the self. Other keywords for this trump are – addictions in general including addiction to people; joy, emotional pain, Insomnia, turn problems in to jokes, inner peace.

- Geranium, bergamot and lavender essential oils are a good choice from aromatherapy to help to find and understand the self, help to deal with addictions and will provoke the necessary changes to a person met the physical and spiritual balance. Fennel and Eucalyptus teas are very recommended as well.

- To balance this figure, the advice from Dr. Bach list is Agrimony Flower Essence.

Agrimonia Mantra: 'I find the peace with myself. I accept whom I am and seek for changes to be a better person every day. I release all the emotional pain and set my 'self' free to live a life of joy.' – From Paula Tooths' #mymantratoday

"The jovial, cheerful, humorous people who love peace and are distressed by argument or quarrel, to avoid which they will agree to give up much. Though generally they have troubles and are tormented and restless and worried in mind or in body, they hide their cares behind their humor and jesting and are considered very good friends to know. They often take alcohol or drugs in excess, to stimulate them and help themselves bear their trials with cheerfulness." – **Dr. Edward Bach**

42 – POPULUS

- This card had the inspiration on a well-known British tree called Populus tremula (Salicaceae), also common in freezing areas such as Scandinavia and Finland. Popular medicine, uses the substance reduces swelling/ inflammation because of the salicin that is in it. The bark and the leaf are very much used in allopathic medicine because of the chemical, which is very similar to aspirin. Medicines for rheumatisms, back troubles, prostate discomforts, neuralgia and bladder problems are made from this tree all around the world.

- Populus represents a paranoid mind that often is afraid with no reason. Fear of the known and the unknown. The long-term challenge will be to see clearly and be perceptive of intuitive information. Probably, most of the situations this draw is perceived as a fear, it is related to the future and what it can't see crystal clearly, causing agitation, often from a previous emotional trauma in the past. Commonly by talking in sleep.

- Quite, rarely shares the problems with others and never takes the risk or accept an adventure. Very sensitive and equally imaginative, other keywords for this Mandala are routine, trust, faith, hope, understanding, phobia, anxiety, apprehension, panic, vague, unclear, lack of direction, irrational and superstition.

- This trump must use aromatherapy to set all the fears free. Roman chamomile, rose, lemon and sandalwood notes can bring the confidence back. If they use all together as a blend, it can rescue the emotional imbalance. Chamomile tea every night before bed may aid the understanding of the fears and release them.

- In order to harmonize the psychic forces of this figure, the advice from Dr. Bach list is European Aspen Flower Essence.

Populus Mantra: 'I set myself free from all fears and feel love instead. I am filled with courage and inner strength. I am confident and open to new life experiences.' – From Paula Tooths' #mymantratoday

"Vague unknown fears, for which there can be given no explanation, no reason. It is a terror that something awful is going to happen even though it is unclear what exactly. These vague inexplicable fears may haunt by night or day. Sufferers may often be afraid to tell their trouble to others." – **Dr. Edward Bach**

43 – FAGUS

- The inspiration for this Mandala comes from the tree Fagus sylvatica (Fagaceae). The nuts were rendered into soap and the nut's oil used for cooking and lighting. The bark in ancient times used to carve symbols and later to write books and painting. Interesting that the runes, that once was a Scandinavian alphabet that had been created to translate the bible, it was made from this tree. The Celts had the belief that this plant could make anyone stronger. In Homeopathy, Fagus has a massive importance in treatments of epilepsy, vertigo and migraines.

- This card represents criticism and intolerance to others. The sense of superiority sometimes blinded by the mirror making this figure quite arrogant and judgmental. Fagus believes that they own the right and others point of view appears always to be blocked.

- Tense is Fagus. Allowances here can be a big challenge as much as create a positive attitude. Impatient and with no much sympathy to the others, other keywords related to this trump are inflexible, routine, over care, concern, rigid posture, indifference, lack of acceptance, fixed, grounded and control.

- Vetiver, Patchouli and lavender scent can help to release this resistance and create more harmony to the self. Lemon and mint added in meals in drinks might aid to deal with tolerance, causing a spiritual awaken.

- European Beech Flower remedy is the best pick from Dr. Edward Bach list. It will help to create more space to flexibility and find more love and joy in life.

Fagus Mantra: 'I release the feelings of judgment and criticism. I forgive others as I forgive myself. I accept differences in the ways of others.' – From Paula Tooths' #mymantratoday

"For those who feel the need to see more good and beauty in all that surrounds them. And, although much appears to be wrong, to have the ability to see the good growing within. So as to be able to be more tolerant, lenient and understanding of the different way each individual and all things are working to their own perfection." **- Dr. Edward Bach**

44 – CENTAURIUM

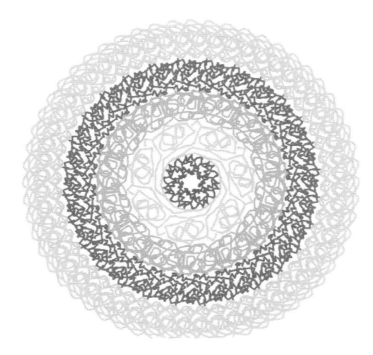

- Inspired on the plant Centaurium erythraea (Gentianaceae) that has blooming flowers during the European summer. This plant been named after Centaur Chiron, the Greek mythological who had innumerous cure abilities. In the old days, Centaurium was famous already to be a strong antioxidant and be a perfect poison to solve gastric and liver problems. In homeopathy, the aerial parts have a big importance on anorexia and dyspepsia treatments.

- Centaurium represents the shy, timid and vulnerable figure. Emotionally week, its enable to say no, as much is the one enable to say negative things even if it comes as a comment against others. Have really poor definition of their own.

- Hard worker always follows the orders given. Obey every topic on the policies. This card is very sharing what makes it neglect their true wishes and consequently, the goals as well. Other keywords linked to this trump are kind, gentle, pale, tiredness, abusive relationships, lack of ability.

- To help this Mandala, the herbs will narrow to black pepper and chamomile to be added in drinks and meals. The science of aromatherapy recommends scents, which touches the trough chakra in particular. Good choice will be sharp notes of basil, spearmint and spearmint.

- Dr. Bach studies would appoint to Centaury Flower Essence in other to improve the strength and grab for confidence.

Centaurium Mantra: 'I am the master of my life. I serve others been true to myself. I confidently follow what I know to be right for Me.' – From Paula Tooths' #mymantratoday

"Kind, quiet and gentle people who are over-anxious to serve others. They overtax their strength in their endeavors. Their wish so grows upon them that they become more servants than willing helpers. Their good nature leads them to do more than their own share of work, and in so doing they may neglect their own particular mission in life" - **Dr. Edward Bach**

45 – CERATOSTIGMA

- This card was inspired on the Ceratostigma willmottiana (Plumbaginaceae), originated from Tibet. It has a blue bloom during the autumn and turns red after the season. Used in traditional Chinese medicine to treat rheumatic problems, as much as in western homeopathic medicine.

- Ceratostigma represents the self-confidence and a handful of abilities. Very firm on own decisions, talk-active, this figure establishes concentration, focus and discipline. This trump virtue is wisdom.

- Certainty is the main keyword, but intuition is a good adjective for this trump. Always open to create security and provide emotional support. Ceratostigma understands that in life nobody needs the others approval. The long-term challenge is to deal with a hidden core personality.

- Juniper, grapefruit and vetiver are the essential scents that aromatherapy calls the attention for. For this mandala, used separate or as a blend they will bring more confidence, relax the body and the spirit, underline the spiritual lessons and establish the needed harmony.

- Cerato flower remedy will be the choice from Dr. Bach list to balance the confidence, certainty and cut out all of distrust of ability.

Ceratostigma Mantra: 'I release all my doubts. I trust in my own inner guidance. My focus and concentration promote a perfect line between my goals and I.' – from Paula Tooths' #mymantratoday

"Those who have not sufficient confidence in themselves to make their own decisions. They constantly seek advice from others, and are often misguided" – **Dr. Edward Bach**

46 – PRUNUS

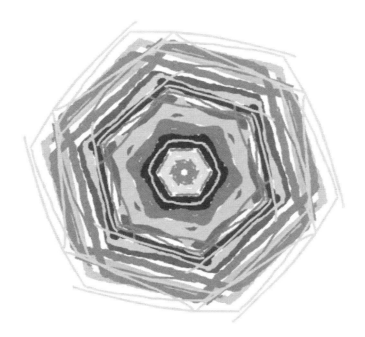

- The inspirations sweetly appear from Prunus cerasifera (Rosaceae), an ancient Chinese tree with gold-rose fruits, this centuries later has been spread in Europe. Homeopathy and Asian popular medicine uses that blooming tree to deal with psychosomatic emotional issues.

- This Mandala represents the control. It works well under pressure. Always will be attempted for alcohol and drug dependency, what will make this a life time of challenges.

- Alive figure, anger rarely appears with this trump. Over-thinking and multitasking, other keywords related to this card are knowledge, spiritual resources, courage, hard word, fear free and abusive controlling.

- In aromatherapy, to calm the mind and rescue the control of the self, its recommended scents as lavender, peppermint, vetiver, mandarin and chamomile. Also, to make a massage or a self-massage using one of the single essential oils just mentioned or all blended in sunflower carrier oil will promote an absurd relief.

- Cherry Plum Flower Remedy is a good choice on Dr. Bach list to keep all under control and release the fear.

Prunus Mantra: 'I release what is tight and let it become light. I keep calm and in peace even under pressure. I remain balanced under extreme stress.' – from Paula Tooths' #mymantratoday

"Fear of mind being over-strained, of reason giving away, of doing fearful and dreaded things, not wished and known wrong, yet there comes the thought and impulse to do them." **- Dr. Edward Bach**

47 – AESCULUS

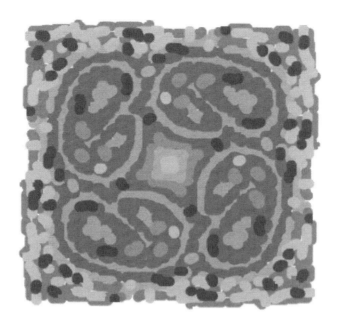

- Aesculus hippocastanum (Hippocastanaceae) was the tree that was the inspiration for this mandala. Aesculus has various interesting aspects. The nuts are well known to become a kid's game: conkers. Also, it has a very soapy juice, this was important to wash and whitening fabric and materials in the past. It produces a strong sort of acetone, which is produced for the military armaments. In medicine, it's very important to prevent vascular problems. It's the world's favourite when the subject is to admire bonsais.

- This card represents stubbornness. Usually this figure is disable to learn from experiences from itself life or even observing others mistakes. Sometimes feels like the memory is so short, that its like burning the hands on the fire and just a few minutes later put the hands there again gaining a new scar.

- The big challenge for this trump is learning – this means in the school, friends, relationships, business and yet the immune system, causing longer time for physical illness to be cured. The memory is short, that helps a lot the forgiven. Sometimes, the thoughts can be confused and will appear as a blockage on the answers in every single aspect of life. The main keyword for this figure is immaturity.

- Aromatherapy will go directly to rosemary essential oil, which will help activate the memory, see clear the past and the understanding that the mistakes aren't to be repeated.

- Dr. Bach flower remedy most advised for this Mandala is white Chestnut Bud essence, which will aid the understanding of the ones mistakes, to those to not been repeat.

Aesculus Mantra: 'I learn the lessons of my life experience. I release my guilty for my mistakes and I forgive myself. I changed my thoughts, now I have a new life.' – from Paula Tooths' #mymantratoday

"For those who do not take full advantage of observation and experience, and who take a longer time than others to learn the lessons of daily life. Whereas one experience would be enough for some, such people find it necessary to have more, sometimes several, before the lesson is learnt. Therefore, to their regret, they find themselves having to make the same error on different occasions when once would have been enough, or observation of others could have spared them even that one fault." **- Dr. Edward Bach**

48 – CHICORIUM

- This card was inspired on the blooming blue flowers of endives - Cichorium intybus (Asteraceae), also known as blue daisy or blue dandelion. Coffee substitute, ancient German medicine uses the leaves in weight loss and skin treatments and the modern medicine uses it to deal with gastric problems. The plant also has a giant veterinary importance to cure warms.

- This card represents the love; the unconditional love. The challenge for Chicorium's life is to learn to love and respect without have a favour paid back. Usually it doesn't understand the emotional value of things, address material principles always as priority and push's back feelings. It can be a very suffocating card.

- Very careful and with the need to have the control of all, this figure has a massive difficult to show affection and consequently can push away people around. Possessive, over-protective, self-centred, critical, nagging, self-pity, easily offended, manipulating, demanding are other keywords linked to this trump.

- Unconditional love and self-love can be developed when one appeals to aromatherapy, choosing scents as Patchouli, Orange, Ylang Ylang, Lavender, Mandarin. Using it all together as a blend in the ambient or directly to the skin can provoke a life transforming.

- On Dr. Edward Bach sciences, the best pick will be Chicory flower essence that will help the figure to me more affective and it will improve the unconditional love within.

Chicorium Mantra: 'I respect the freedom of those I love. As I let go I will find love and security lies within. I trust my worthiness to love and be loved. My love is unconditional.' – From Paula Tooths' #mymantratoday

"Those who are very mindful of the needs of others they tend to be over-full of care for children, relatives, friends, always finding something that should be put right. They are continually correcting what they consider wrong, and enjoy doing so. They desire that those for whom they care should be near them" **- Dr. Edward Bach**

49 – CLEMATIS

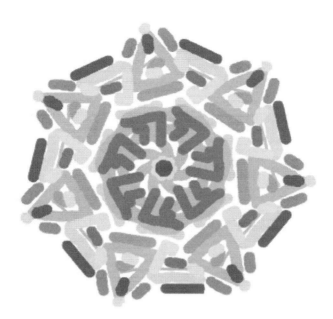

- Inspired on the bright white flowers of Clematis vitalba (Ranunculaceae), it can be a plantation to suffocate if not looked after. In homeopathy, it is commonly used in high potencies to cure varicose and ulcers in general. In Chinese traditional medicine, it is used as antimicrobial and anti-inflammatory.

- This Mandala represents the creation of the soul. It can be daydreaming and count with lack of focus and low ability of concentration. Connections are hard to establish. It's like a person living in a bubble, almost as an autistic child who can't connect with the external world.

- Problems to keep attention may occur. Time to rethink reality with careful organisation and timings. Lifetime challenge to this card is discipline to concentrate on the real, diverting the attention to is so important. Keywords related to this trump are absent, missing feelings, over thinking, superficial, cursory, shallow, surplus, and pointless.

- Scent notes as geranium, cedar wood and patchouli will help the one to be present and grounded, promoting the real awaken and connect with the reality with a clear view. The kitchen is in need of the critics, which is advised to adding in meals and drinks.

- Clematis flower remedy can be interesting for this figure, to create a cosmic integration with the 'self' and fit a link between the dream and the reality.

Clematis Mantra: I am free to focus on my present circumstance. I am present in this real joyful world. I can see clear my need and goals now. I work with focus and concentration in all aspects of my life. – From Paula Tooths' #mymantratoday

"Those who are dreamy, drowsy, not fully awake, no great interest in life. Quiet people, not really happy in their present circumstances, living more in the future than in the present; living in hopes of happier times when their ideals may come true. In illness some make little or no effort to get well, and in certain cases may even look forward to death, in the hope of better times; or maybe, meeting again some beloved one whom they have lost." - **Dr. Edward Bach**

50 – MALUS

- Inspired in the old English wergulu, fruit of Malus sylvestris (Rosaceae), one of the nine plants invoked in the 'nine herbs charm', part of the traditional pagan Anglo history. This is supposed to cure the physical body and the soul. This fruit, a red-golden apple is very important in European literature on subjects where there is hidden beauty described, what is believed is it comes from the European pagan witches to make potions and spells, to make enchantments to bring love, beauty and prosperity. Because the various properties as laxative, nutritive, antibacterial and anti-inflammatory, medicine uses it in treatments of the trough, the eyes, digestion problems and weight loss programs.
- Malus represents cleansing. Usually, this figure has a poor self-image and poor view about the self. Also it can be noticed that its traits include maniac compulsive obsession for cleaning and organization. Or in extreme cases, this card can appear following cases of anorexia or other emotional disorder illness.

Emotional tense and over anxious, this trump can maximize obsessions. Can see clearly the reality of others, but when the subject is the 'self' then can fail for believe to be "less" or "smaller" then really is, affecting largely the self-esteem. Other keywords for this mandala are lack of purity, despair, despondency, lack of acceptance, fussy, purity, lack of spirituality, irritability, shame, oversensitive and perfectionism.

- The feeling of personal imperfection and dirtiness can be improved with aromatherapy. Sage, palmarosa, lemon and black peppermint essential oils are highly recommended. In the kitchen, adding apple of all sorts and black pepper can help to reach the purity.
- The best pick on Dr. Edward Bach list is Crab Apple flower remedy. It will aid the purification in both bodies: the physical and spiritual, finding finally harmonious peace.

Malus Mantra: 'I feel clean and harmonious. I accept my imperfections as a lesson. I am perfect just as I am. I am clean of all negative thought and I can see clear now the true perspectives.' – From Paula Tooths' #mymantratoday

"This is the remedy of cleansing. For those who feel as if they have something not quite clean about themselves. Often it is something of apparently little importance: in others there may be more serious disease, which is almost disregarded compared to the one thing on which they concentrate. In both types they are anxious to be free from the one particular thing which is greatest in their minds and which seems so essential to them that it should be cured. They become despondent if treatment fails. Being a cleanser, this remedy purifies wounds if the patient has reason to believe that some poison has entered which must be drawn out." **- Dr. Edward Bach**

51 – ULMUS

- Inspired on the very strong English tree Ulmus procera (Ulmaceae). Later, this tree travels to Asia becoming a very popular choice on the art production of bonsais, where also is used as an ant parasitic. Western medicine uses Ulmus to treat anxiety, compulsive behaviours, obsessive thoughts, and peculiar mental impulses.

- This Mandala represents responsibilities. The responsibility here can so many times be crashing the figure that needs to look forward to balance all the chakras. Full of self confidence, this card doesn't understand its own limits when to stop to take more tasks, being always over worked.

- Very capable trump, try to take the responsibilities of others and unneeded ones, losing the spiritual balance. Exhausted and can have a temporary lack of self esteem and can be prone to depression and anxiety crises on periods of overload, starting to doubt of itself goals. Keywords are: despondent, tiredness, stress, inadequacy, search of spiritual balance and self-assurance.

- Aromatherapy will point to geranium, rose, frankincense and bergamot essential oils, for moments when you feel overwhelmed; to help to cope and release what is unnecessary.
- English Elm flower essence from Dr. Bach list will aid to set free the feeling of be overwhelmed and unprepared. It will provoke a spiritual and physical relax and, of course, balancing all; making one understand the real mission of life.

Ulmus Mantra: 'I choose to be responsible. I am confident as I am feeling my life mission. I release the burden of perfectionist striving.' – From Paula Tooths' #mymantratoday

"Those who are doing good work, are following the calling of their life and who hope to do something of importance, and this often for the benefit of humanity. At times there may be periods of depression when they feel that the task they have undertaken is too difficult, and not within the power of a human being." **- Dr. Edward Bach**

52 – GENTIANA

- Inspired in one of the 180 species of the purple flower of Gentianella amarella that has the hit of blooming during the sunny month of September. TCM uses the plant to treat common fevers with flu, thought and lung infections. American natives use it to clear heath problems caused by climate conditions. European Natural Medicine uses the roots to help with emotional psychosomatic situations. And finally, homeopathy works with this plant to treat jaundice, exhaustion, sore thought, depressions, angers, general upsets, digestive problems and appetite loss.

- It is the Mandala that represents faith; it's a very perseverant and confident figure. Never gives up on goals and makes wherever is needed to achieve them. The big life challenge is to keep the self-body free of the depressions, which can lightly occur.

- Gentiana holds lots of courage and it is the trump that works with the faith we carry about ourselves and is a connector to rescue the confidence in our pure state. This figure will tirelessly search for the grace in the earth and the solid spirituality. The mind here is very settled and firm. Positive and strong, other keywords related to this draw are practical, hope, focus, courage, attitude, action, victory, success and, prosperity.

- Aromatherapy advises Bergamot, Lavender, Petitgrain, Ylang Ylang notes to restore the faith and open the life to abundance. Parsley, mint and basil are recommended to adding to drinks and meals; it will aid this card to be more courageous about the goals and follow with greater confidence.

- Gentian Flower essence is the best pick on Dr. Bach list. This flower remedy will treat the lack of faith and it will help to open the portals of the Universe to bring to a person what it is asking with an open heart.

Gentiana Mantra: 'I am confident of ultimate success. I am in line with my goals and with faith I work hard to meet them. I knowledge setbacks as life opportunities' – from Paula Tooths' #mymantratoday

"Those who are easily discouraged.may be progressing well in illness or in the affairs of their daily life, but any small delay or hindrance to progress causes doubt and soon disheartens them." **- Dr. Edward Bach**

53 - ULEX

- Golden furze, the flowers of Ulex europaeus (Fabaceae or Leguminosae) was the inspiration for this trump. Folklore tells that when the gorse is out of bloom, kissing is also out of season; the flowers blooms most of the year. It was important in old herbal medicine to treat jaundice and scarlet fever; for the astringent properties, was much used to help with bowels issues; also a well-known reputation as a good insecticide. Modern herbal medicine use furze to deal with worms. But after all my researches, the most interesting fact I met was in the county side of Ireland, where horologists and alchemists hang the flowers by the door to bring good luck.

- This figure represents the hope and the positive thoughts arriving. This Mandala is able to banish all the negative energy and magically touch all around, giving a renewed positive solution.

- Ulex is the symbol of the eternal light, which guides us to the right and prosperous decisions, to achieve the level of nirvana. Other keywords applied to this trump are hope, stimulation, restore and persuasive. The challenges for this card are despair moments.

- Geranium, Rosewood, Bergamot and Jasmine scents are the tip from aromatherapy to renew the vows of hope with the inner guide. Using all this essential oils together can bring revelations in a reflexology massage. Adding more citric flavors to your drinks and meals on a daily basis can provoke a lift on your physical and spiritual bodies.

- On Dr. Edward Bach sciences, Gorse essence can help this mandala to put it together and start from where it stopped, bringing back hope and faith.

Ulex Mantra: 'I completely trust my inner guide. I remain hopeful despite difficulty. I release all my doubts now and follow my destiny path full of hope and faith.' – from Paula Tooths' #mymantratoday

"Very great hopelessness, they have given up belief that more can be done for them. Under persuasion or to please others they may try different treatments, at the same time assuring those around that there is so little hope of relief." - **Dr. Edward Bach**

54 - CALLUNA

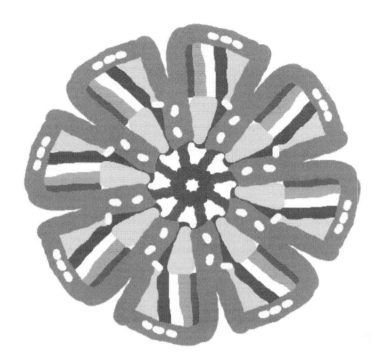

- Inspired on the beauty of the plants Calluna vulgaris, what gives us the delicate flowers, including Cassiope and Erica, one of the eighty species. Herbal medicine uses that plant in treatments of body cleansing and kidney stones. Old alchemists used to make potions promising it could cure rheumatism. Allopathic medicine uses all the parts of the plant on the production of tablets for treatments of menopause and menstrual problems. Also it's common to find species of Calluna on medicines to deal with digestion, weight loss, circulation system and nervous breakdown.

- This card represents the emotional self-sufficiency. Self discovery is made as priority but has a need to this trump are always the center of attention, always needing a crowded – not necessary agreeing with the thoughts. Solitude here appears to be a long-term challenge, but once one wants to solve it, easily can be converted in harmony.

- Very meditative and sociable; Talkative, demand attention, dislikes being alone; lonely are keywords that can be related to that card. This draw rarely became a good listener.

- Aromatherapy narrows to scents as rose, blue chamomile, bergamot and frankincense. Those aromas can be very helpful to help this figure to deal with the dependence in other people.

- Heather flower remedy is the best pick on Dr. Bach list. It will bring some teaching with issues of loneliness like how to deal successfully with it.

Calluna Mantra: 'I believe in myself and trust in my journey. The Power of the Universe flows freely through. In this light, I listen and give to others. Loneliness is transformed into inspirational meditation.' – From Paula Tooths' #mymantratoday

"Those who are always seeking the companionship of anyone who may be available, as they find it necessary to discuss their own affairs with others, no matter who it may be. They are very unhappy if they have to be alone for any length of time." **- Dr. Edward Bach**

55 - ILEX

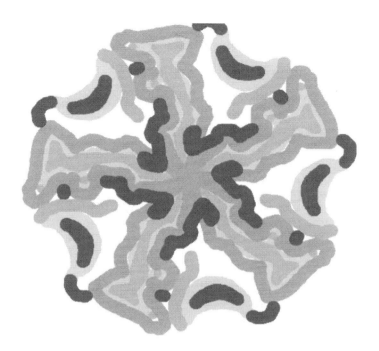

- This Mandala had inspiration Ilex aquifolium (Aquifoliaceae) that holds the famous Christmas berries and leafs. Medicine uses it very carefully because it can be toxic. Its very diuretic, so used in diets with observation; also laxative and integrant of old natural medicine on the treatment of fever.

- Ilex represents the divine love. Challenged to treat to the self without care what others are or have, this card crosses the path trying to proof unconditional love. But the ''purity'' here is not always clear.

- If not spiritually treated, some symptoms can appear for this trump as insecurity, obsession, jealously, envy, suspicious and aggressively. But once the compassion has been understood, life can take track again and be in full harmony. It's a battle to fill up the self, which so many times doesn't feel satisfied because it didn't find yet a real purpose in life.

- Ylang ylang fragrance is traditionally used in aromatherapy to sharpen the senses and to temper depression, fear, anger, and jealousy. Peppermint and rosemary could be added on a daily basis to help the inner awaken to a real purpose and optimize the capabilities.

- Researching Dr. Edward Bach studies, English Holly Flower essence will come up for this card. Compassion will appear naturally and answers about the self will be bring to this figure, making clear hidden abilities and teaching how to be more giving.

Ilex Mantra: 'I have real purposes for my life. I encourage and give strength to others. I feel gratitude for the good will of others. Compassion makes my life flows easier.' – from Paula Tooths' #mymantratoday

"For those who are sometimes attacked by thoughts of such kind as jealousy, envy, revenge, suspicion. For the different forms of vexation. Within themselves they may suffer much, often when there is no real cause for their unhappiness." **- Dr. Edward Bach**

56 – LONICERA

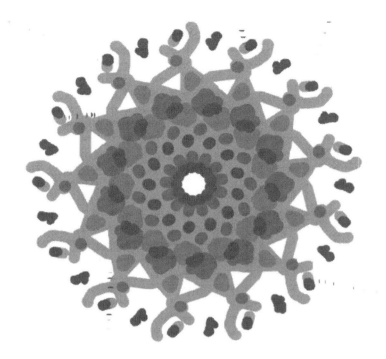

- This draw was called after the plant Lonicera caprifolium (Caprifoliaceae) because it is qualified as magical in so many natural medicine lineages and philosophical beliefs. Indications start on fever and summer heat, furuncles, diarrhea, problems with toxic blood,

- This Mandala symbolizes the link with the past, taking a bit of the joy that this figure suppose to be living on the present time. Its full of energy and enthusiasm but has to understand the lessons of the experiences and look forward.

- Nostalgic, always is linked to some memory from the past, doesn't matter if it's good or bad. Homesickness, other related words to this trump are bereavement, broken heart and lack of acceptance in life.

- In aromatherapy, some notes can be very useful to help to release the past, letting all the traumas go. Scents as blue tansy; ylang ylang, lavandin and geranium will give to Lonicera the needed strength to carry on strongly. Lots of emotional frames and in Chinese medicine it's called a fairy dust of the diets and detox.

- Honeysuckle flower remedy is the highly advised with this trump. This essence will activates the interest on the present and release past traumas.

Lonicera Mantra: 'The past stands behind me and the future is in front of me. My life is full of presence. I am centered on my present. I am very happy here and now' – From Paula Tooths' #mymantratoday

"Those who live much in the past, perhaps a time of great happiness, or memories of a lost friend, or ambitions which have not come true. They do not expect further happiness such as they have had." **- Dr. Edward Bach**

57 – CARPINUS

- Carpinus betulus (Corylaceae) inspired this mandala, taking back to the Scottish mythology. Mother of Caledonian Forest was the Guardian of land mysteries and history and it is called one of the three trees of life. Homeopathy uses this tree to deal with fatigue, exhaustion and often the feeling of tiredness. The classic medicine treats anxiety. Carpinus were a first aid for old witches who used the leaves to stop bleeding and heal wounds; also they were used in the old Roman Empire to make their chariots because of the strength of the wood.

- Hornbeam represents the energy. Very euphoric and full of energy, can cause fire wherever this card appears. Some around felt enthusiastic and joined this positivism and higher level, but others will feel jealous and the envy can make an individual feel mentally broke down.

- Satisfaction is a life challenge. Sometimes it can be stressful. The whole world won't fill up this trump, because it is a seeker and has a hunger for life. Procrastination can happen, but lots of other positive keywords can be found related to this draw as excited, strength, multiple activities, doers, over thinking, multi tasking, out of routine, innovative and fully involved.

- In aromatherapy, it is massively advised notes of Lavender, Petitgrain and Frankincense. Those essential oils used as single scents or all as a blend can relieve the 'Monday morning' feeling. In the kitchen adding lime, lemon, acai and parsley to meals and drinks can help to release the lack of strength and awake the body and they seek for spiritual revelation.

- Dr. Back found a special flower essence. Hornbeam remedy releases the fatigue, restores dynamic mental and physical energy and will help you regain enthusiasm when you feel dull.

Carpinus Mantra: "I have all the energy I need. I fill my daily tasks with courage and joy. I am interested and involved in all that I do. I move on enthusiastically." – from Paula Tooths' #mymantratoday

"For those who feel that they have not sufficient strength, mentally or physically, to carry the burden of life placed upon them; the affairs of every day seem too much for them to accomplish, though they generally succeed in fulfilling their task. For those who believe that some part, of mind or body, needs to be strengthened before they can easily fulfill their work." – **Dr. Edward Bach**

58 - IMPATIENS

- Native to the Himalaya, Impatiens glandulifera was used in ancient China as a nail varnish and in the other side of Asia, as hair colouring. Traditional purpose of fingernail and hair dying was to scare the bad spirits. American native Indians used to make a potion using the flowers from this plant to treat bites from insects but in particular bees stings. So many pharmaceutics industries uses the balms from this plant to produces shampoos that calms difficult hair. Classic medicine and homeopathy take the advantage of the walleriana species to produce healers for skin problems and anxiety.
- Patient and sensitive, this trump represents the inner peace. Generally bright, fast worker, gentle spirit and nurturing. Prefers to execute tasks by itself so not to take the risk to slow down the final results.

- Full of energy, can cause sometimes a busy and stressful environment. The long-term challenge is to find the harmony point to the temper and look after it closely so as not to explode. The life is always in a rush. Competent in over standard, this Mandala has other keywords: criticism, pressure, deadline, time, quick, stress, indigestion, lack of sleep and disappointment with others pace.

- In order to improve points as intolerance and impatience, aromatherapy can help when point to Camphor, Blue Chamomile, Marjoram, Lavender and Rosewood essential oils. Those scents will calm the spirit and may help with tension and irritation. On the kitchen adding Chamomile and Fennel to drinks and meals can aid immediately relief the tension.

- As the name of the card, the best choice on Dr. Edward Bach list will be Impatiens flower essence to deal with inner restlessness.

Impatiens Mantra: "I embrace life and circumstances with greater ease and flexibility. I am breathing with each moment. I am in harmony with life flow." – from Paula Tooths' #mymantratoday

"Those who are quick in thought and action and who wish all things to be done without hesitation or delay. When ill they are anxious for a hasty recovery. They find it very difficult to be patient with people who are slow as they consider it wrong and a waste of time, and they will Endeavour to make such people quicker in all ways. They often prefer to work and think alone, so that they can do everything at their own speed." - **Dr. Edward Bach**

59 – LARIX

- Larix decidua (Pinaceae) is used in pagan cremation for the waterproof and durable qualities and it's why this sort of pine tree ends up as inspiration to this card. Herbal medicine uses a decoction of the bark to help skin treatments, as eczemas and psoriasis. Native North Americans have used infusions of the needles or bark to treat urinary tract infections as well as respiratory problems. According to Yoga philosophy, it is attuned to the spiritual properties of inspiration, the voice of the heart, and protection.

- This Mandala represents the confidence in its self. It ditches the voice of failure and the feelings of fear. It's the will power that never lets climbing to achieve goals stop. Learn and calculate risks are a challenge to Larix.

- Balanced figure, full of positive expectations, teach others to heal feelings of inferiority. Courage probably is one of the best qualities for this trump. Other keywords linked to this lamina are potential, decision, superior; fear free, talkative and high esteem.

- Cardamom, juniper, lemongrass and rosemary essential oils will be the advise from aromatherapy to invigorate the confidence and increase the energy. Asparagus, centella asiatica and gooseberry added to the Kitchen will stimulate the brain, promotes relaxation, energy and vitality; clear mind and enhances confidence and self-esteem.

- Dr. Bach list will directly point to Larch flower remedy. It will help to gain confidence and follow in a creative and secure way.

Larix Mantra: "I take risks and gain more confidence. I find success in growing from each experience. My energy open all the doors to I achieve my goals." – from Paula Tooths' #mymantratoday

"For those who do not consider themselves as good or capable as those around them, who expect failure, who feel that they will never be a success, an so do not venture or make a strong enough attempt to succeed." **- Dr. Edward Bach**

60 – MIMULUS

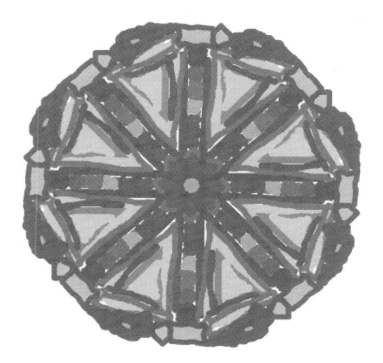

- Mimulus guttatus (Scrophulariaceae) is the plant responsible for the well-known flowers of the yellow monkey flower and ruby jack. Bitter and very salty, Native Americans of the West used this plant as a salt substitute. Folk medicine uses the foliage to treat burns and skin problems. Homeopathy and medicine applies to many uses, but the most often are stress/ nervousness, obesity, diabetes and general system recovery.

- Mimulus lamina represents the fear free of the facts of the life, With courage enough to run and manage the journey. This figure can front shy and timid moments, but easily can track back. Good speaker, always have a ready script for any situation.

- Privacy lover, new situations are always very welcome. This card deals pretty well with anxiety and the worries that may appear during the path. Facing daily challenges is an adventure to this mandala. Affirmative, positive, responsive, prompt are other keywords that can be related to Mimulus.

- Aromatherapy can be supportive with this trump. Jasmine, clary sage, chamomile and neroli essential oils or notes in products that you can adapt or introduce in daily basis will aid a figure to have the courage to find new parts of the Self, flowing in radiant light, very responsive to the new reality.

- Dr. Eduard Bach presents a remedy with identical name to this mandala – Mimulus flower essence, which is amazingly efficient in all cases of fears and phobias.

Mimulus Mantra: "I recognize each difficulty as an opportunity for growth. I act with courage and inner strength. I accept my life experience as I release all my fears." – from Paula Tooths' #mymantratoday

"Fear of worldly things, illness, pain, accidents, poverty, of dark, of being alone, of misfortune. The fears of everyday life. These people quietly and secretly bear their dread; they do not freely speak of it to others." **- Dr. Edward Bach**

61 – SINAPIS

- Inspired on Sinapis arvensis (Brassicaceae), plant that combine with the beautiful charlock flowers. Naturopathy uses that plant to move/ remove scars, in particular to genetic skin problems as keloids, but very carefully because it can be toxic if used in large dosage. Homeopathy applies that tincture to remove emotional scars and physical burns, as much with general congestions, as the respiratory for example. Ancient Russian folklore believes that charlock flower cooked with garlic was their magical potion that could cure anything

- Full of serenity, grace and peace of mind, this lamina represents the happiness with no reason. Its balanced, the understanding and gratitude just to be. Interest excessive in present circumstances.

- Hopeful and using the faith as a tool to achievements, this trump is very prone to the euphoria. It's a strong figure that doesn't let down itself for anything. Extroverted, provides a sort of balance around itself and brings courage and lots of joy to life.

- Aromatherapy can be supportive with experiencing heights and depths. Scents as orange blossom, patchouli, mint and vanilla essential oils may balance the whole. Cinnamon and ginger are highly recommended to adding in drinks and meals, responding as uplifting, to both spiritual and physical bodies.

- Mustard flower remedy is the best choice from Dr. Bach list to this mandala. This essence helps dispel the gloom by allowing in light and joy.

Sinapis Mantra: "Pleasure and pain are part of my journey; Sorrow is optional. The light and the darkness are in total equilibrium creating the color of my soul. I have faith in my process of growth and integration. I choose to live full of joy." – from Paula Tooths' #mymantratoday

"Those who are liable to times of gloom or even despair, as though a cold dark cloud overshadowed them and hid the light and the joy of life. It may not be possible to give any reason or explanation for such attacks. Under these conditions it is almost impossible to appear happy or cheerful." **- Dr. Edward Bach**

62 – QUERCUS

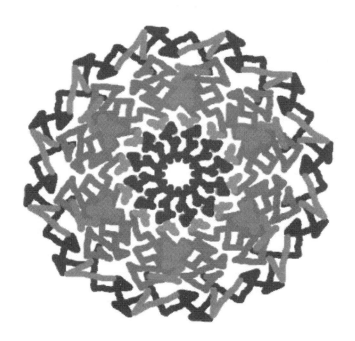

- Quercus robur (Fagaceae), old national emblem of England, took the inspiration for this lamina. King Arthur's roundtable was made from a single cross section of this tree. The druids could cancel a ritual which didn't have this tree on the land, the same rule was followed by the Celtic witches. In German, this tree symbolizes the poetry and romanticism. In folk Irish medicine, because of the astringent properties, a potion made as a tea as used to cure diarrhea and other issues with digestive/ gastric organs. According with the North American natives, the dry leaves can heal blistering, bites. On south American ancient philosophies, Carrying any piece of the oak draws good luck to you but is important to remember to ask permission to the Goddess tree and show gratitude always.

- This trump represents the balance between work and the rest. It's the understanding of the limits of this figure. Sovereignty, leadership, power, full of strength and endurance, this card is almost a warrior. Kind, with lots of generosity and always ready to keep the others around protected.

- Workaholic; overworked, extra hours, lack of sleep, justice, nobility, honesty, bravery are keywords that fits well to this card. Stress and exhaustion will be a lifetime challenge. Relaxing time is needed!

- To rejuvenate the body and vitalize the mind, aromatherapy advises Canadian spruce needle, cedar wood, peppermint and Petitgrain essential oils. Adding to the kitchen lots of citrus on meals and drinks will deport forever the fatigue and stimulates a new view to get on without cross the limits.

- English Oak flower remedy is an interesting pick to this mandala. It will help to cope with exhaustion and to enhance energy to follow strong even when struggling.

Quercus Mantra: "I feel power and passion for life. I feel strong and very energetic. I release the struggle and I experience renewed strength and stability." – from Paula Tooths' #mymantratoday

"For those who are struggling and fighting strongly to get well, or in connection with the affairs of their daily life. They will go on trying one thing after another, though their case may seem hopeless. They will fight on. They are discontented with themselves if illness interferes with their duties or helping others. They are brave people, fighting against great difficulties, without loss of hope of effort." **- Dr. Edward Bach**

63 – OLEA

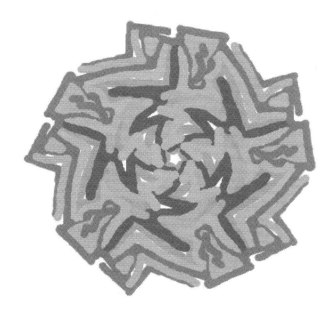

- Mediterranean, Olea europaea (Oleaceae) is the most cited tree in the whole literacy history. Famous to be the wood used to make the sculpture of the mythological Greek Gods. The legend says that all the olives, fruits of this tree, disappear in the land when the Persians attacked Athens, and it grew up in the same very day as a miracle, when the olives become sacred to the Greeks. The tree is mentioned over 30 times in the bible and a few times on the Torah. Classic and natural medicine uses the fruit and seed oil to present heart diseases and breast cancer, cure skin issues, high cholesterol, bloody pressure unbalances, strokes and rheumatic frames.

TOOTHS / MANDALA LIFE COACH

- This lamina represents endurance. With an internal reserve of strength, full of energy, this figure is never tired. Always ready to the next task. Competitive, own an incomparable force.

- Gold health, other keywords can be read with this trump are efforts, active mind, physical strength, vitality and leadership. This mandala can cope well with extra duties and has good abilities to carry with stressful work.

- Recommended adding olive oil to the kitchen to assure health is kept in top levels. A hot cup of infusion made of orange peel; cloves and cinnamon can be very useful to this Mandala. Elemi, basil, ginger, rosemary and Chinese mint essential oils are the advice from aromatherapy to boost the energy and avoid tiredness.

- Olive flower essence builds strength and endurance after physical or mental exertion. So, this remedy will be the choice from Dr. Bach sciences for this draw.

Olea Mantra: "I make conscious use of all my energy. I relax and experience a new strength within me. I become whole again." – from Paula Tooths' #mymantratoday

"Those who have suffered much mentally or physically and are so exhausted and weary that they feel they have no more strength to make any effort. Daily life is hard work for them, without pleasure." - **Dr. Edward Bach**

64 – PINUS

- Inspired by the European Christmas tree Pinus sylvestris (Pinaceae) with incomparable fresh balsamic scent, associated with dwelling places of fairies and gnomes, and thought of as benevolent, refreshing places where tired walkers can safely rest in the protective aura of the tree. The pines from this tree are used as an amulet, to revoke protection and call prosperity. In Lebanon, its symbol of immortal life. In folk medicine its called "transfer magic"; intending to avert any emotional or physical pain back to the mother tree. Pineal gland was called after the pine, and naturopathy says that is where the seat of the soul is. The whole tree is medicinal, between the properties its anti-inflammatory, imunostimulant, antiseptic and anti-rheumatic and very useful in many treatments for the respiratory system.

- Pinus lamina represents the forgiveness. It teaches to make strong the self, make one understand the experiences and how to take the best lesson of it.

Inadequacies are according to interpretation, principles, values and point of views. This card is able to find all the possibilities of joy in life.

- Gently figure, softness and serenity are strong characteristics to represent it. Master who spreads peace, tranquility and calm. Other important keywords to this trump are resilience and determination.

- British Red Pine, after all the presentation with no doubt is the best choice on aromatherapy. The resinous aroma permeates the air and each breath one takes is like sipping nectar, invigorating body and soul. It elevates the spirit, clears the mind and makes the feet move lightly along the path. Pine kernels are very restorative and fortifying… Think about to at least try it!

- Dr. Edward Bach also worked hard studying this tree. Taking Pine flower essence will help to accept the self, releasing all the guilty and setting free the past mistakes.

Pinus Mantra: "I free myself from inappropriate guilt and blame. I understand and forgive. I love and accept myself. I see new possibilities and move forward." – from Paula Tooths' #mymantratoday

"For those who blame themselves. Even when successful they think they could have done better, and are never satisfied with the decisions they make. Would this remedy help me to stop blaming myself for everything?" **- Dr. Edward Bach**

65 – AESCULUS CARNEA

- Inspired by the tree Aesculus carnea (Fagaceae), which is already a cross between two other species of chestnuts. It was trying to produce massive and colorful kernel nuts that biologists generate this tree in France in the 18th century. In old days, the Arabs would dye with wine, but they couldn't find a way to enlarge the local nuts. Naturopathy studies the properties still but defends that the fruit of this tree has cleansing function and can take off poison from a human body.

- It's all about courage and belief the representation in this draw. This mandala worries excessively about the family needs and friend's problems, what so many times make it forget about the its self.

- Compassion and humble; fraternal love and protection are the main sets of words to this trump.

- Aromatherapy highly recommends lavender, ylang ylang, bergamot, May chang, neroli and rose essential oils to aid with a healthy detachment from the problems of others. Blend all together and using it in a massage and meditation moments with bring a coat of protection of feelings and relaxation, magically!

- Red chestnut flower remedy from Dr. Bach list must be a very best pick increasing the capability to cope with stress, stop to over care about others and look inside the self to watch the real needs; and releasing fear of future.

Aesculus Carnea Mantra: "I remain calm despite my concern for others. I send blessings to others. I am radiating peace, calm, and optimism. I love to meditate and look into myself inner voice." – from Paula Tooths' #mymantratoday

"For those who find it difficult not to be anxious for other people. Often they have ceased to worry about themselves, but for those of." - **Dr. Edward Bach**

66 – HELIANTHEMUM

- Oklahoma symbol, Helianthemum nummularium (Asteraceae) produces flowers known as cistus, which marked the territories of the natives Cherokees, meaning on their legend the edge or the end of the path. The flowers are well known to become sculptures of crystal when forgotten for centuries. Folk medicine uses the flowers to deal with respiratory problems and treatments to nervous system. Classic medicine classifies the flower as anti-viral, anti-bacterial, stimulates immunity and alchemists make a special re-birth potion because it stops hemorrhagies very quickly.

- This trump represents the internal emotional torture. Traumas that are forgotten and the figure do not want to think about or let it go either. The mandala symbolizes a shock (physical or emotional) that is begging for a review and asking the possibility to be released.

- Clearly, this trump is finding difficulties to stay centered and remain grounded to effectively deal with challenging circumstances. Keywords that can be remembered for this read are immobility, physical trauma, rigid body, speechless, hysteria, panic, phobia, fear and anxiety.

- Aromatherapy advises neroli, Melissa and camphor essential oils. This notes will aid when one feeling that cannot react or move, finding the needed courage and the center self to deal with freeze fear moments.

- Called panic button essence, Rock Rose flower remedy from Dr. Bach list, will re-create the calm and helps one to let the negative feeling to go and move forward.

Helianthemum Mantra: "I am a light warrior spirit. I deal big challenges with faith and bravery. I cross all the problems firmly and grounded with my self-transcendence. " – From Paula Tooths' #mymantratoday

"The remedy of emergency for cases where there even appears no hope. In accident serious or sudden illness, or when the patient is very frightened or terrified, or if the conditions is serious enough to cause great fear to those around. If the patient is not conscious the lips may be moistened with the remedy." - **Dr. Edward Bach**

67 – SOLARIZED

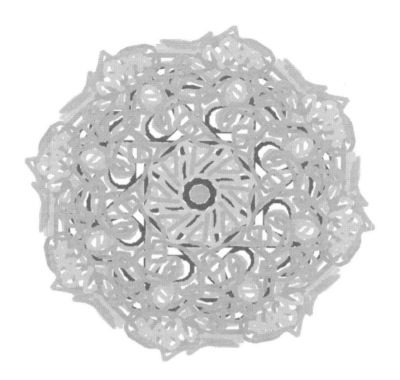

- This Mandala isn't just my favorite but in my opinion on of the most important on the last group. Historically, Dr. Edward smartly settled the 38 essences in groups. But was his loyal assistant who realized and reported that the energy of the blossoms was transferred to the water. Taking this fact to the corner, he took time to seriously research the spring waters of East Britain. In conclusion, he provided to the world the information of the healing properties of the solarized water, which was coming from the rocks in that area.

- This lamina symbolizes the flexibility of our thoughts, our emotions and even our terrestrial body. The long-term challenge here is to try not to become dominated or be transformed in martyr or victim. Follow routines, polices and regular habits, but doesn't permit the self to became a slave of it. The card understands that it always can have a solution 'out of the box' or an escape that nobody else is open to.

- Kind and generous figure, Solarized has a pretty logical view of life. As water that flows in the ocean, this lamina has the same properties, which make for this trump main keywords: flexibility, receptivity and spontaneity.

- Aromatherapy blend of marjoram, roman chamomile, cypress, helichrysum, lavender, and juniper berry can be very useful to cases when it is needed to adapt, overcame and improvise. Sage, coriander and mint added to drinks and culinary in general will add and relax to understand the self and achieve some flexibility.

- Rock water flower remedy, even is the unique Dr. Bach essence it isn't made from a blossom but made of solarized spring water, it is the recommendation for this Mandala. It is indicated to the ones who are inflexible, keeping rigid standards.

Solarized Mantra: "I Transform all my strength in flexibility. I open my mind and my heart to new experiences. I flow with life dancing the melody of the stars, in line with my feelings." – from Paula Tooths' #mymantratoday

"Those who are very strict in their way of living; they deny themselves many of the joys and pleasures of life because they consider it might interfere with their work. They are hard masters to themselves. They wish to be well and strong and active, and will do anything, which they believe will keep them so. They hope to be examples which will appeal to others who may then follow their ideas and be better as a result." **- Dr. Edward Bach**

68 – SCLERANTHUS

- The inspiration comes from the wild flowers of German knotgrass, Scleranthus annuus (Illecebraceae Caryophyllaceae), which is very mutant and grows in self-fertilization. In Europe, with it just flowering during summer and because the plant is a very sandy lover, adapts better closer to the sea, Used by ancient pagans to offertory rituals to the moon. African tribes use the fruits for speelworks and spiritual rituals of evocation of Gods. Natural medicine uses that plant to combat infection, diabetes, hypertension and relief stress. Traditional Chinese medicine uses that plant as a potential diuretic, in particular in diet and detox programs.

- This Mandala symbolizes certainty. The emotional balance is stabilized with this draw. Easy to make the mind because it holds knowledge, which doesn't leave any doubts to remain. Definetely not a time waster.

- Clear and open mind, good memory and wisdom are good keywords to run with this lamina. This trump has complete control of the mood and because it's supportive, appears as a good leader.

- In order to remove indecisions and release doubts, aromatherapy indicates spikenard and cedar wood essential oils to this trump. Help with low mental clarity and set free emotional confusion.

- Named exactly as this lamina, Scleranthus flower remedy from Dr. Bach list, is the recommendation. This bloom essence can help to find balance on the self and reach the ability to make decisions.

Scleranthus Mantra: "I grow every time that I decide to take a risk. I take chances and I make choices. I always choose de direction through to the true" – from Paula Tooths' #mymantratoday

"Those who suffer much from being unable to decide between two things, first one seeming right then the other. They are usually quiet people, and bear their difficulty alone, as they are not inclined to discuss it with others." - **Dr. Edward Bach**

69 – ORNITHOGALUM

- Inspired on Ornithogalum umbellatum (Liliaceae), the flower that the florists and followers calls the symbol of purity, reconciliation and atonement. It has a really long shelf life, and holds a symbolic biblical meaning. It was the guide of the wise man to find Jesus's birth. In Greek mythology, starting with the botanical name, it means 'something incredible to happen'. In homeopathy, it is to be considerate in cases of digestive problems, intestinal cancer, and lots of stomach ailments, as gastric treatments and even when hemorrhages occur. Yet, very much associated to occult rituals and pagan potions to evoke rebirth.

- This card represents comfort. Shows clearly that this comfort was learnt from heavy traumas from the past, temporary shocks or some considerable loss. This figure became an expert in comforting people because it needed to learn in the hard way and provide the healing to the self.

- Lying back and very giving, nothing can put down this trump. It's unity and relief from the most troubling of situations. To the self and others around. Soothing, other keywords related to this mandala are stress, worries, over caring, overthinking, over-reacting. The life challenge to this frame is leaning to let go, and past traumatic moments in special.

- In aromatherapy, Lavender, Geranium, Lemon and Clary Sage essential oils can be very supportive to track back with balance. It will replace the sorrow with joy. Can be very helpful, adding to the drinks and meals in regular basis, some chamomile, asparagus ginseng and mint; this recipes will help the feelings, healing quicker the trauma scars.

- Star of Bethlehem flower remedy, the most potent healer on Dr. Bach essences list is the recommendation to this lamina. It will promote a relief of a trauma and bring some emotional comfort when needed.

Ornithogalum Mantra: "I release all traumas from my past. I believe on the strength of my star. I feel calm and soothed. I find comfort to my soul when I am really enjoying life. I feel renewed every moment that I permit my star to shine." – from Paula Tooths' #mymantratoday

"For those in great distress under conditions which for a time produce great unhappiness. The shock of serious news, the loss of someone dear, the fright following an accident, and such like. For those who for a time refuse to be consoled, this remedy brings comfort." - **Dr. Edward Bach**

70 – CASTANEA

- In the old Roman Empire, Castanea sativa (Fagaceae) was used to construct the monasteries in that region that's why this tree came as inspiration to this Mandala. The nuts soon become very popular in Europe to produce a very particular sort of sugar and with time crossing, the nuts became an indispensable recipe in the kitchen in a big variety, including thick flour. Very much used in folk medicine with the promises to be a fortifying which could cure any illness. Himalayan popular medicine uses all the parts of the tree, barks and leaves is special; according with this culture, it can help with diarrhea and all stomach complaints, infections, hemorrhages, kidneys and muscles problems, bronchitis, rheumatic condition and fever.

- This lamina symbolizes the faith. The lifetime challenges to this figure is between the faiths and feel strangled by its 'God'. The fear is present personage of its life, who often finds hiding the self behind facts, excuses, people or even things. This can provoke a personality "fake" enthusiastic.

- Castanea draw can be found related to addiction as drugs and alcohol, or in the worst of the cases in apologizes. Lack of endurance, stress and exhaustion can became keywords to this trump, that needing right now faith, hope and strength to believe that it can do without help. This card finds difficulties to focus on the present and establish positive thoughts.

- Aromatherapy can be supportive with notes as bergamot, frankincense, rose and clary sage essential oils to comfort feelings of despair and loneliness. Adding to the kitchen oat, rosemary, clove, ginger, thyme, lemon and ginseng when the soul is tested by periods of dark despair; those recipes will promote a new light to the path.

- Sweet Chestnut flower remedy will be the advice from Dr. Bach list. This essence will help the 'self' to reconnect spiritually, refocusing life on happiness and joy; fostering spiritual depth it instills the faith that we can overcome adversity through spiritual communion.

Castanea Mantra: "I appreciate the blessings of the present life. I find courage and faith in a divine power. My faith encounters Spirit through aloneness." – from Paula Tooths' #mymantratoday

"For those moments which happen to some people when the anguish is so great as to seem to be unbearable. When the mind or body feels as if it had borne to the uttermost limit of its endurance, and that now it must give way. When it seems there is nothing but destruction and annihilation left to face." - **Dr. Edward Bach**

71 – VERBENA

- Verbena officinalis (Verbenaceae), called 'tears of Isis' by Egyptian Mythology, has long been associated with divine rituals and supernatural powers. Because it is well known as a re-connector with the self, since early years, writers believe it is a mind opener and drink teas of this plant to un-block. Old pagans used that specie for abortions. Homeopathy commonly uses it in cases of melancholia, depression and nervous exhaustion; Naturopathy applies it for migraine, fever, respiratory illness, dental treatments and jaundice. In traditional Chinese medicine it's indicated for system cleansing. The classical medicine sees the plant related with success in gastric and anxiety treatments. The holy herb, which is also named, was the main flower on Druids' altar ritual.

- Moderation is calling! This lamina represents fixed principles and ideas. Righteous indignation is the belief system of this figure. The lifetime challenge will be about the understanding that the self-truth isn't unique; that other people may be right as well. Very reluctant in credit a life slot to deal with inner peace; Open the mind (and sometimes the heart) it's the best advice for those.

- Competitive, fast talkers and fast movers, this card doesn't leave much space to flexibility. Over caring, over concerning, Over-enthusiasm, hyperactive, obsession, fanatical, highly strung is main keywords to this card. Argumentative, trying to persuade everybody around. Verbena has the feeling "I'm always right", difficultly can be turned in a leader with loyal followers.

- To relax the 'type A personality' that characterize Verbena, aromatherapy can be supportive. Adding in regular bases scents as Basil, Juniper, Passionflower, Rosemary and Clary sage essential oils. It will help this trump to be more flexible and be more understanding.

- Vervain flower remedy is the best pick from Dr. Edward Bach list. This essence can help to balance this powerful energy and teach the tolerance to approach life with more harmony.

Verbena Mantra: "I see with open mind into my experiences. I accept the gift of life when I am accepting myself. I allow others to follow their beliefs in their own way. I can let others be." – from Paula Tooths' #mymantratoday

"Those with fixed principles and ideas, which they are confident are right, and which they very rarely change. They have a great wish to convert all around them to their own views of life. They are strong of will and have much courage when they are convinced of those things that they wish to teach. In illness they struggle on long after many would have given up their duties." – **Dr. Edward Bach**

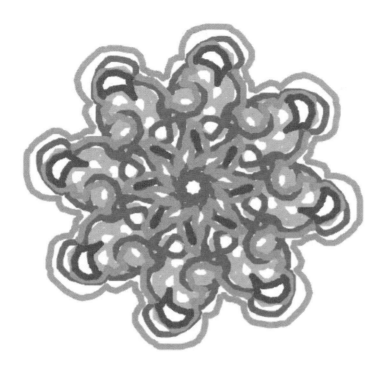

- Vitis vinifera (Vitaceae) have always been in the history of the human being. On the Gods' rituals and Christ chalice, grapes describe civilizations. Folk medicine knew already the importance of this plant and uses in ancient cosmetics and to treat skin diseases. These days, Vitis is applied to so many types of tumours and in extreme cases as cancer. Diarrhea, trough infections, uterine problems and joints crises are treated with it as well.

- This card is efficient, ambitious, grid, strong willed, and as a gamer, keep studying to give the appropriate orders, but in some how always mange to lead others with success. Vitis is gifted with natural power and brings to itself others obedience without limits.

- Authoritarian, this trump loves power and will do anything to gain more. When it loses the interest in someone, they can be very cruel, and show tension with no control. Highly capable, other keywords can be linked to this lamina are selfish, stress, tyrant, ruthless, willful, dramatic, gesticulation, nervousness, spoil and bullying.

- Promoting the recognition in the values of others and their thoughts, aromatherapy recommends coriander, Melissa, orange blossom, myrrh, geranium and ylang ylang essential oils. Using all as a blend, it will bring forgiveness, acceptance and healing now!

- Vine essence is with no doubt the best indication from Dr. Bach list. This remedy will show some relaxation and carry some humility into a life of this card,

- Vitis Mantra: "I learn leadership by embracing others' goals. I become more powerful through spiritual service. My will power is in balance with the power of the Universe. I accept myself when I am accepting the beauty in everyone's differences. " – From Paula Tooths' #mymantratoday

"Very Capable people, certain of their own ability, confident of success. Being so assured, they think that it would be for the benefit of others if they could be persuaded to do things as they themselves do, or as they are certain is right. Even in illness they will direct their attendants. They may be of great value in emergency." **- Dr. Edward Bach**

73 – JUGLANS

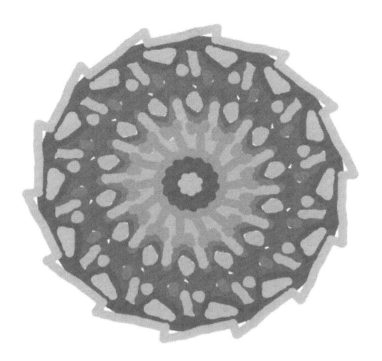

- In the Golden Age, the Greeks believed that the Man lived in the acorns and the Gods slept inside the fruit of Juglans regia (Juglandaceae). According to Arabic-Indian folkloric history, it is an aphrodisiac, used to cure cancer, rheumatism, growth, indurations, tumors, warts, intestine, kidneys, lip, liver, mammas, mouth, stomach, throat issues and uterus. Old European pagans never left home without a nut of it in the neck – it could put away the evil big eyes!

- Juglans in the father of the changes and it is here to symbolize and protect all the transitions. From this card comes the lesson that it's breaking free from the past, which is what make us strong in the future. The challenge for this mandala is to be careful to don't let the pressure make negative influences in times of changes. Just watch the vulnerability of the self.

- Emotional stabilized, other words, which can appear for this lamina, are puberty, menopause, pregnancy, death, new life, life changing, divorce, wedding, retirement, moving and beginning/ ending of a relationship.

- Aromatherapy recommends cypress, balsam fir, lemon, grapefruit and geranium notes. Those essential oils may be very supportive in transitions, promoting protection from outside influences and energies. In the kitchen, naturopathy advises adding garlic, ginger, cinnamon and mint to drink and meals; making changes emotionally easier.

- The best choice on Dr. Edward Bach list to enable to make easy transitions in life is English walnut flower remedy. It generally helps us to break free from the past and move forward with confidence. The essence also is indicated to those professionals who daily deal with sadness and tragedies.

Juglans Mantra: "I see my inner power into new experiences. I now have the strength to follow my own inner guidance. I welcome new opportunities. I ditch limiting thoughts. I release all the negative influences from the past." – from Paula Tooths' #mymantratoday

"For those who have definite ideals and ambitions in life and are fulfilling them, but on rare occasions are tempted to be led away from their own ideas, aims and work by the enthusiasm convictions or strong opinions of others. The remedy gives constancy and protection from outside influences." **- Dr. Edward Bach**

74 – HOTTONIA

- Hottonia palustris (Primulaceae) is a flower that is usually given as a gift meaning dedication and loyalty. Eastern European witches relate that flower as a spice of potions; just need to emerge it into blessed water, vinegar or tea. Pagans of Roman Empire used to make syrup of Hottonia flowers, water and sugar, which could heal the soul. Always related to magic and rituals, on actuality, this plant is used to manufacture handmade 'dream pillows', relaxing baths after magic rituals, and spell works.

- This Mandala represents sharing. Full of wisdom, this lamina likes the isolation, often to read or study and grab more knowledge. Its self sufficient and self contained. Its not a figure of so many friends, but just a few well chosen, it will be kept forever. A very sensitive soul full of natural born gifts that needs to share with others. Extremely reserved, the main keywords here is independent, self reliant, private, aloof, anti-social, disdainful, condescending, lonely, lack of humility and need for others. Funny enough, everybody seeks Hottonia advices.

- This card bears pain and sorrow in silence, rarely will share it and this frame brings up the life challenge – its absolutely something to be learnt! This lamina feels lonely because they have a tendency to appear proud and anti-social.

- Palo santo, Clary sage, roman chamomile, frankincense, bergamot and helichrysum essential oils can be very supportive to this trump. Aromatherapy advises then to relax the feeling of loneliness, teaching gradually the art of sharing. The Universe needs to hear about its gift!

- Water Violet essence is the choice on Dr. Bach list. This remedy helps Hottonia to open and share their gifts, becoming more inclusive rather than exclusive and open the soul to connect with others and appreciate social relationships.

Hottonia Mantra: "I am open now to share and appreciate others. I am sharing my love and wisdom. I seek connection because the world needs me. I recognize love in my Self when I'm sharing love with others." – from Paula Tooths' #mymantratoday

"For those who in health or illness like to be alone. Very quiet people, who move about without noise, they are aloof, leave people alone and go their own way. Often clever and talented. Their peace and calmness is a blessing to those around them." - **Dr. Edward Bach**

75 – AESCULUS HIPPOCASTANUM

- Traditionally the leaves and bark of Aesculus hippocastanum (Hippocastanaceae) are used as a tea, and can also be used to make tinctures, creams, and infusions, and commonly found as cough syrup. The whole nuts are poisonous and are only to be used for external application, but very much picked from cosmetology manufacturers. In old days, the Turkish people used to treat their horses with respiratory problems with the flower from this tree, originating the name 'horse chestnut'. Homeopathy applies this tree to deal with haemorrhoids, varicose veins and venous insufficiency. Classic medicine often uses the tree for the high properties as anti-inflammatory and antioxidant. In Europe in particular, it's used for rheumatic and kidneys treatments. Pagan's

185

studies say that specie can make a Botox effect and witches says that this is the tree of reverses – a person can prepare a potion for the good or the bad.

- Aesculus represents the tranquility. It symbolizes the calm and balanced mind. The life term challenge to this figure is to learn how to ditch unwanted negative thoughts and never permit that those keep round and round on the mind. Mental arguments can happen, but as said, it is daring to send they away. Because this Mandala is full of concentration, this effort can cause insomnia, agitated sleep & dreams and sleeplessness. Controversial, this card never gives up. Other words linked to this trump are repetitive, routine, chatter, overactive, temporary anxiety and with some training Aesculus H. can be turned in a Zen spiritual leader.

- Aromatherapy recommends cedar wood, lavender and roman chamomile essential oils promoting calm, peace and inner quite, useful before bed. It can help with insomnia, sleeplessness and agitations.

- White Chestnut flower remedy is the indication from Dr. Edward Bach list. This essence will help to find answer to the situations allowing less mental effort, also may promote the ability to unwind.

Aesculus Hippocastanum Mantra: "When my mind is empty, the divine can speak. I am quite and balanced within. I release anxiety and all negative thoughts. I seek peace." – from Paula Tooths' #mymantratoday

"For those who cannot prevent thoughts, ideas, arguments which they do not desire from entering their minds. Usually at such times when the interest of the moment is not strong enough to keep the mind full. Thoughts which worry and still remain, or if for a time thrown out, will return. They seem to circle round and round and cause mental torture. The presence of such unpleasant thoughts drives out peace and interferes with being able to think only of the work or pleasure of the day." - **Dr. Edward Bach**

76 – BROMUS

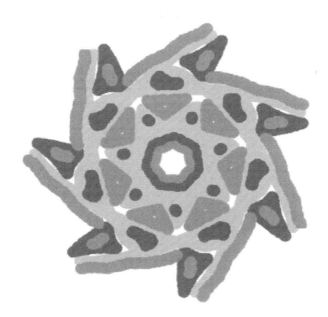

- Well known as aphrodisiac, Bromus ramosus (Poaceae) was the inspiration for this Mandala. Herbalism indicates it to the heart because they keep blood fats under control. Soothing to the brain and nervous system, often Bromus is used in expensive tablets related to impotence. Medicine recommends for skin problems and anxiety as well. Avena sativa, how is popular called, is a regular recipe for PMS, exhaustion and sleep treatments.

- This lamina is an eternal seeker, who finds sometimes lack of direction. Doubts about work and carrier can affect this figure, that sometimes find difficulty about certainty in relationships as well. Naturally a life challenger and love new adventures.

- Ambitious, constantly bored with present life, avoid commitments; but once this trump focus the energy can be anything wants in life because it has so many talents. Keywords can be fitted to this reading are self-actualization, self-esteem, awaken, spiritual connection, goal breaker and lack of ability to find a niche in life that promotes full satisfaction.

- Promoting integration of higher and lower aspects of consciousness, aromatherapy advises cinnamon bark, ginger, black pepper, sandalwood, nutmeg, rosewood, patchouli and sage essential oils. These scents used as single or together in a blend, will help to express the real life purposes.

- Dr. Bach studies will point to Wild Oat essence. It's the flower remedy to help to find the true direction in life and improve the belief within. Generally, stimulates interests in life.

Bromus Mantra: "I have faith in the direction I choose. I am very clear about my goals. My inner guidance shows me how to move forward. I create and attract new opportunities every day." – from Paula Tooths' #mymantratoday

"Those who have ambitions to do something of prominence in life, who wish to have much experience, and to enjoy all that which is possible for them, to take life to the full. Their difficulty is to determine what occupation to follow; as although their ambitions are strong, they have no calling which appeals to them above all others. This may cause delay and dissatisfaction." **- Dr. Edward Bach**

77 – ROSA

- With miraculous properties Rosa canina (Rosaceae), is the flower of Venus, Goddess of Love and Beauty. Folklore mentions that this flower can keep the eternal youth and beauty. The wiccans use this rose to evoke spirits and ask for their helps. Homeopaths prescribe Rosa to patients with urinary difficulties and bladder affections. Chinese medicine is investigating it still for controlling cancer growth. Rosa canina hips are very popular all around the world to be turned in tea, jam, jelly and marmalade.

- Very alive, this card symbolizes the fire, the romance, the lust, the enthusiasm. The type of the figure that 'make the day'; if isn't perfect, it will find perfectness into simplicity. Life never is monotonous or boring.

- Improver and restorer, hungry for life, very interested and never let the self down. This trump finds energy and enthusiasm even when nobody else can find it. Other keywords important to understand this lamina are quality, hope, faith, strength, light, role model, beauty, renewal, joy, happiness, abundance of energy and uplifting.

- Juniper berry, orange blossom, Clary sage, peppermint, black pepper, amyris and ylang ylang essential oils will create a celebratory uplifting, providing the necessary vitality to embrace life in full. Used in ancient prayers, Rosemary probably is the herb it can cause best effect in the kitchen. Adding sarriette, oregano, parsley, cardamom, thyme and ginger to drinks and meals can be very useful to this lamina, says Herbology studies.

- Wild Rose essence is the match on Dr. Edward Bach list. This flower remedy claim to stimulate interest in life, designing new goals and fighting for it with vitality.

Rosa Mantra: "I embrace my life with joy. I develop new and positive life goals every day. I express my vitality in my challenges. I turn life resignation into interest and enthusiasm." – From Paula Tooths' #mymantratoday

"Those who without apparently sufficient reason become resigned to all that happens, and just glide through life, take its as it is, without any effort to improve things and find some joy. They have surrendered to the struggle of life without complaint." **- Dr. Edward Bach**

78 – SALIX

- Salix vitellina (Salicaceae) is a tree most associated with the moon, water, the Goddess and all that is feminine. It is the tree of dreaming, intuition and deep emotions. The old precursor of 'aspirin', this plant is used in Chinese medicine for thousands of years, it can immediately low a fever and relief deep pains as classic medicine applies to inflammation cases. Homeopathy uses the Salix tincture to deal with Fitness and Sports Injuries. The pagans, uses Salix to make the ritual of surrender, reconnect to the duality of the light and the dark, emotions and unconscious and to balance the main elements of nature.

- This lamina represents flexibility. Optimism and full of sense of humour; arrogance and vanity doesn't fit in this figure existence. Very forgiven, Salix is a guru who teaches forgiveness wherever it goes. Always this card admits mistakes and instead to turn it into bitterness or see the self as a victim, look move forward and learn with the experiences. Laughs of the own mistakes and uses then as a lesson.

- Salix has feeling for others and it's a good coach. Stimulates optism in all environments. The challenge of life is to learn give some value to material things, because this card is completely unattached. Enjoy friendships and like to share smiles. Other keywords related to this draw are quality; blame free, fear free, fair, judgment free, responsibility, balance, harmony, spiritual connector and wisdom.

- Aromatherapy can balance the feelings and foster flexibility, acceptance and forgiveness when advises palmarosa, angelica, Melissa, neroli, petitgrain, lotus flower, lavender, blue chamomile and jasmine essential oils. Old Hindu studies says that adding turmeric, cardamom, basil and ginger to the kitchen will connect this trump and bring the understanding to move forward with real joy.

- Golden Willow essence is the recommendation from Dr. Bach sciences, helpful for treating envy and resentment towards others whose success, prosperity or happiness we desire. This flower remedy also will aid with forgiveness, including the self.

Salix Mantra: "I forgive and share my blessings with others. I accept the responsibility for my life. I take responsibility for my thoughts. I release the guilty feeling and move forward. I turn bitterness into positive attitude." – from Paula Tooths' #mymantratoday

"For those who have suffered adversity or misfortune and find these difficult to accept, without complaint or resentment, as they judge life much by the success which it brings. They feel that they have not deserved so great a trial that it was unjust, and they become embittered. They often take less interest and are less active in those things of life which they had previously enjoyed." - **Dr. Edward Bach**

* * * * MANDALA JOKER 1/2 * * * *

- Eripio is a word that in old Latin means 'rescuing out'. The inspiration to this Mandala comes from the lesson from the Universe that all of us born to be. It's an emergercial and necessary rebut on the self-system, to it be back to the genuine purity.

- This card represents our souls, out of the negative thoughts, free of fears, able just to love unconditionally. The purity of the deep self. The will power to leave all behind and attend to the real desires, to serve the propose of life that the figure burn inside but do not follow because do not think its met with society or family principles or wishes.

- Time to release all traumas, pains, fears and negativity. It's the opportunity that the soul was calling to be naked to recreate, improve and move forward with prosperity.

- A blend of wild lily, musk and sandalwood essential oils is the tip from aromatherapy science. Believing that it can be the yoga in a bottle, it will awake the true self, captive the senses and ground the emotions. Instincts and intuition are the worth keywords to this transition.

- Magical dilution of Helianthemum nummularium, Clematis vitalba, Impatiens glandulifera, Prunus cerasifera, Ornithogalum umbellatum essences, composing the five flowers remedy from Dr. Bach list is the recommendation to this lamina, backing the figure to the center, in line with the universe.

Eripio Mantra: "I am positive energy. I am uplifted and confident, happy just being me. I find harmony in the divine guidance. I cultivate unconditional well-wishing and open-hearted nurturing of my Self and others." – From Paula Tooths' #mymantratoday

"Health depends on being in harmony with our souls" – Dr. Edward Bach

* * * * MANDALA JOKER 2/2 * * * *

- Inspired on the legendary pilgrimage of Joseph of Arimathea bringing the chalice of Jesus' last super to be hidden on the spring waters of Chalice well in Glastonbury aggregating the power of the Latin word 'sentio' which means 'to feel', 'to experience', 'to perceive'. Full of magic, history, spirituality and knowledge that comes by previous generations.

- This card symbolizes rich overflowing abundant source of a life force energy. It also shows that everything and everybody is correction allowed. A challenge here can be the understanding of second chances can happen just permit the self to look around using the eyes of the heart and feel the answers to arrive.

- Time to review principles and values; time to meditate! This lamina is a lift to move forward, renewed, in rhythm, in harmony, in balance, using the sunshine as a melody. Very joyful and wise, also the creator of a whole new understanding of the earth and all its relations. Other keywords we can relate to this lamina are courage, occultism, cleansing, balance, good vibration, retreat, religion, connection, spiritual journey, growth, re-birth and nirvana.

- Aromatherapy will point to a wise blend of cypress, Bergamot, Black Pepper, Chamomile, Clary Sage and Lavender essential oils to release the feeling to be stuck or lost in the dark and improves access to the soul through. In daily basis, the body and the soul are requesting more pure spring water to be added.

- Seeking alignment with the earth and all its powers, the richness of the Universe and its abundance, a good choice in Dr. Bach list is a blend of crab apple, oak and holy flower remedies.

Sentio Mantra: "I am divinely guided in all I do, say and think. My soul, mind and body are in complete alignment with the Universe. I choose to clearly understand the higher messages within my dreams and intuition. I clearly recognize and embrace any and all signs from the Universe. I am divinely guided in all I do, say and think. " – From Paula Tooths' #mymantratoday

"There is no such thing as a true tale. Truth has many faces and the truth is like to the old road to Avalon; it depends on your own will, and your own thoughts, whither the road will take you." - Marion Zimmer Bradley

MANDALA: ARTE OR DIVINATION?

Mandalas have been used for thousands and thousands of years. In ancient empires as Egyptian and Persian, oracles had paintings on the floors and some times on the roof, representing different things depending on the culture, and on the center of these 'Mandalas' that speakers and meditators would make a world of the Universe into their words and like they said to the followers or crowd how the future is going to be, what was coming and what would happen and how to sort or continue on.

In some Indian creeds, a Mandala in the old days could determinate a lineage of a politician or a kingdom.

The practice of creating Mandalas as a sacred art and spiritual science of consciousness originated many thousands of years ago in India, as believe the most of the scientists, but the rumours are many. Yantra, for the traditional Hindus, was the 'machine' of healing. Using the centre called 'bindu', which means absolute; the meditator could leave the material world into meditation and experience unity, balance or try the nirvana state.

In Tibet, the sand Mandalas are very symmetrical and include geometric shapes, sacred draws, spiritual icons and deities of this region. A Tibetan Mandala comes as 'art therapy', in order to heal the individual who was executing the work with sand, creating a unique piece and with the vibration and prayers, also healing the community. The Australasian aborigines had a similar ritual, which later was substituted for tree barks and natural paints.

In Navajo sand paintings, as in Aboriginal art, images are not symbolic in the usual sense of the word, but always refer to specific elements existing in either physical or mythological

197

space. The North American natives created their sand paints to be used in healing rituals and called them wheels, was there where the native healers would find the problem and the solution to deal with. Many native people and pagans use the Medicine Wheel, a Mandala form, to connect to earth energies and the wisdom of nature.

Japanese Buddhism has a special tradition with Mandalas too. The 'Womb Realm' and the 'Diamond Realm' exoteric rituals, both to initiate Shingon Buddhism students.

Chinese Buddhism uses a paper hanging scroll called moji-mandala, where a mix of Chinese characters and medieval Sanskrit scripts represent elements of the religion. Mahayana Buddhism, precursor of Taoism and Bön, traditional in east Asian countries, uses medieval Mandalas provides a visual representation of the Pure Land texts, and is used as a teaching aid. Some lineages of Buddhism use a Mandala in the home altars to meditate into the prayers.

Mandalas appear in the complex patterns of Islamic art. The old Jewish history, says that the circle represents the female and the square represents the male, remembers Maagalot as Jewish Mandalas relate not only to the circle but also to the square and to their shared centre. The rabbi would stay in the centre and pray. And of course, the Star of David, symbol of Hebrews.

Christians count with Mandalas exposed into sacred architecture all over the world. Evocative forms of Mandalas are prevalent in Christianity – rosary, Christian cross, Celtic cross, rosy cross, rose windows, crown of Thorns, oculi, aureole, halo and the most of sacred pieces of arts and paints in floors, roofs and walls. Mandalas also can be found in draws of Rosicrucianism, exoteric Christianity, hermetic, and Christian alchemy.

Mandala house is the name of one of the 16 Druid historical buildings Heights. It is a construction is a shape of a flower of Lotus.

Triquetras, spirals, knots and lots of others Celtic symbols of holy trinity, exoteric, protection and love. Scientists believe that the new generation know a very small percentage of Celt tradition Mandalas and their symbology; but with no doubt, Mandala is very present on this folklore.

Psychologists who follow Jung, have the strong belief that a mandala "a representation of the unconscious self," and using this draws its possible to define a wholeness of an individual; personality or a disorder of a person. Professor David Fontana, also psychologist, defended "it's symbolic nature can help one to access progressively deeper levels of the unconscious, ultimately assisting the meditator to experience a mystical sense of oneness with the ultimate unity from which the cosmos in all its manifold forms arises."

There are so many the meanings and forms Mandalas can be found. In my beliefs, even a body of a human being, animals and elements so the nature is forms of Mandalas.

I couldn't finish this book without mentioning the crop circles. Some believe that they are a liberate scam made from farms; others believe it is a spiritual connector or a message from other worlds. One or other, those circles are beautiful forms of Mandala, used to meditate, as a divination and subject of studies. Wherever, it is a brilliant connector, because keep people talking about, studying together and trying to find explanation that maybe, just maybe, it's much bigger than us.

One thing I can say – Using Mandalas with faith and orientation, miracles can come to our encounter!

The best day of your life is the one on which you decide your life is your own. No apologies or excuses. No one to lean on, rely on, or blame. The gift is yours - it is an amazing journey - and you alone are responsible for the quality of it. This is the day your life really begins. ~ Bob Moawad

FINAL NOTE

I do not advise aroma therapeutic essential oils or Dr. Bach Flower Remedies/ Essences been taken during the pregnancy, breast-feeding or to the ones under the legal age.

Nothing I wrote here is intended to be medical advice. Follow my recommendations at your own risk or make an appointment with your regular doctors.

I absolutely wish to be helpful to the ones who are interested in divination and some how this book will bring some answers or positive information to you all. This journey that I have completed wasn't to be just a tool to the ones who are seeking for the art of divination, but I expected to be useful and prepare with the cards, a guide to introduce Ayurveda, yoga, aromatherapy, Herb ology and homeopathy, yet all the other therapies studies I collected from all the places I been during my life.

May the long time sun shine upon you, blessing our lives now and release all the pain and any fears.

Wishing that each one find your miracle journey....

And with peace, that your commitment be your destiny.

Peace to all,

Paula

"May the Guide light illuminate me to teach others with the knowledge I learnt during the past years help their paths.

May the Angels make me an instrument to change this world and introduce some relief to the families in sorrow.

May the Universe bring to me some ability to dry the tears and provoke smiles in the darkness.

May the Mother Earth pass to me the keys of the pain and see on it the needed answers.

May the Gods give me a hand to guide people to follow fascinating histories

May all my prays during all those nights, makes true to me the dream to help humanity to find their deep inners and meet it with their souls"

– Paula Tooths

Paula Tooths H.I.Dip. is Journalist and Producer, Bachelor in Information Technology, has Higher International Diploma in Naturopathy and Psychotherapy (Int. in Hypnotherapy and Past Life Therapy), Acupuncture and Homoeopathy.

Also studied Advanced Nutrition, Herbalism, Iridology, Aromatherapy & Cosmetology, Shiatsu and Ayurvedic Medicine. Recently, finished her studies in Coaching.

Paula born in Sao Paulo during the late 70's from an Italian family and has lived for a decade in England.

Printed in Great Britain
by Amazon